A Faith
Worth
Sharing

Also by C. John Miller

Powerful Evangelism for the Powerless
  (available from P&R Publishing)

Come Back, Barbara
  with Barbara Miller Juliani
  (available from P&R Publishing)

Outgrowing the Ingrown Church

Repentance and Twentieth Century Man

A Faith Worth Sharing

A Lifetime of Conversations About Christ

C. JOHN MILLER

P U B L I S H I N G
P.O. BOX 817 • PHILLIPSBURG • NEW JERSEY 08865-0817

Unless otherwise indicated, Scripture quotations are from
the King James Version or the author's own translation.

Scripture quotations marked (NIV) are from the HOLY
BIBLE, NEW INTERNATIONAL VERSION®. NIV®. Copy-
right © 1973, 1978, 1984 by International Bible Society.
Used by permission of Zondervan Publishing House.
All rights reserved.

Typesetting by Michelle Feaster
Page design by Tobias Design

Printed in the United States of America

Library of Congress Cataloging-in-Publication Data

Miller, C. John, 1924–1996.
    A faith worth sharing : a lifetime of conversations
about Christ / C. John Miller.
        p.   cm.
    ISBN 0-87552-391-9 (pbk.)
    1. Miller, C. John, 1924–1996. 2. Witness bearing
(Christianity) 3. Christian biography—United States.
I. Title.
BR1725.M446A3 1999
248'.5—dc21   99–28900

To our son, Paul.

*It was Paul's idea that his father write
this book in the last weeks of his life.
He wanted Jack to write down some of
his stories of how he shared the gospel of
grace with friends, relatives, and strangers.
Jack and Paul worked together on many
different projects. Jack wanted to dedicate
this final collaboration to Paul.*

Rose Marie Miller

Contents

Acknowledgments

Because Jack died after he had finished only a rough draft of this book, many people, both family and friends, had a significant part in bringing it to publication. In particular, I want to thank two of my daughters, Roseann and Barbara, who worked many hours organizing and editing this book. I also want to thank Sue Lutz, who did the final editing on the book. Sue has edited all of Jack's books, and it was a special gift from a busy lady when she worked on this final project.

ROSE MARIE MILLER

A Word from the Editors

Dad had a remarkable way of engaging people with the gospel. Some of these engagements took place in predictable ways and places: pastoring churches, writing books, and speaking at conferences.

But there were plenty of unpredictable encounters as well. Dad always felt responsible for the person he found himself next to—whether he was cooking breakfast in a boarding house, having a snack in a Paris café, or collecting trash in Uganda. Over the years we (his children) were the captive audience for Dad's stories about his efforts to share his faith. It became predictable that he would get himself into unpredictable predicaments . . . and regale us with the stories.

This is a book of some of the stories. In the last years of his life, Dad worked hard at writing a book for skeptics. As he weakened physically, it became an increasingly frustrating effort. It was in the real life, person to person encounters that he came to life. Watching Dad's frustration with his current writing project, Paul (our brother), suggested to him that he write down the many different ways he shared his faith. Dad took up the challenge and began to record these stories in the last six weeks before he died.

These are the stories that Dad wanted to leave his family and friends. They are stories of faith begun and faith renewed, stories of how God changed people as they heard the gospel from Dad, stories of his failures and God's successes. As we read this book, we see that it is about the power of the gospel to change anybody—men in a boarding house, college students, drug-addicted hitchhikers, successful businessmen, and even Dad and his own family.

The structure that Dad used to share these encounters is the story of his own life. He weaves together the story of his faith journey with the stories of the many different people he met along the way. But he was not able to complete the book before he died. When we opened chapter 10, we found just two paragraphs. Because Dad left us in the middle of the book, we asked our mother to write an epilogue. It incorporates some of what he wanted to include in the final chapter.

Dad's faith was contagious. To be near him was to get a fresh infusion of faith—and to believe again that God is in the business of changing people. Editing this book was a way for us to be near Dad again. We laughed and cried as we read the stories. It comforted us and changed us. Now it is his (and our) gift to you.

BARBARA MILLER JULIANI
ROSEANN MILLER TROTT
EASTER 1999

Sharing a
New Faith

CHAPTER ONE

San Francisco, 1948

"I'll take it."

The boarding house on Eddy Street was dilapidated on the outside, and worse on the inside. But it offered a job and a place to live, and I needed both while I was at college. So I said to Bill, who owned the place, "I'll take it." With those words I accepted the job of breakfast cook for over a dozen single men.

It wasn't much of a job, and I wasn't much of a cook.

But Bill promised to train me. Early the next morning, under his watchful eye, I burned toast, overcooked eggs, and charred bacon. After an hour and a half, he limped away, grumbling, leaving the smoky battle station to me. Bill was elderly and shaky in health—watching me torch his kitchen had exhausted him.

From now on it would be up to me to master

the art of cooking breakfast for my blue-collar roommates.

After about a week I still burned the toast, but the eggs and bacon were no longer semi-incinerated. Most of the men had a good sense of humor, and some of them even made helpful suggestions about how to time my preparations. Cooking breakfast may sound simple, but doing it for that many men took coordination. It wasn't easy to have the eggs, bacon, toast, and pancakes all done at the same time.

Gus, a fellow student at San Francisco State, helped with the preparation of the evening meal for his room and board. On the basis of his experience, he gave me friendly encouragement every morning. At least as much as I could understand. He was Panamanian, and his knowledge of English was still limited.

Here on Eddy Street I had my first experiences with sharing my faith. I had become a Christian only two months before, while working as a flagman and laborer on a highway maintenance crew in southwest Oregon. Before that I had been a college student in San Francisco. But I had dropped out. I had too many questions that college wasn't answering.

I also think that a difficult childhood had caught up with me. My father had died when I was two years old. My mother remarried and my stepfather made life hard for all of us. I left home at sixteen and went to live with my sister in San

Francisco. While working at the Navy Yard, I earned a high school diploma. About that time, we heard that my older brother Leo, who had protected and befriended me after my father died, had been killed in the war.

This news left me confused and searching for answers. I made my way back to my hometown in Oregon, and I got a job working on the highway and spent my spare time reading the Bible. Although I had been an atheist for many years, I couldn't stop studying the Bible. Eventually God met me while I was wrestling with Ephesians, a small book in the New Testament. Reading it turned my world upside down. I had come to the end of the road, where there is nothing left but God. But he was all I needed.

Now I was different. Rather than being self-centered and self-absorbed, I had a new center—a relationship with my Father in heaven. Now I had a hunger to live for my new Father. I longed to share the joy that had come to me when my life was surrendered to God.

For me to know Christ was to know joy. It seemed to me that people were missing out on the best thing in life—not knowing about the love of God and the splendor of my Savior. I returned to school in San Francisco eager to share this new faith. I wanted to introduce everyone I met to my Father in heaven, knowing that the real changing of the inner life had to be the work of his Spirit. I knew that was the only way a stubborn person like me could come to God.

Now on Eddy Street, I wanted to share my faith with the men I cooked for, but they were not at all religious. At least three were outright atheists. They were not easy to talk with, especially about matters of the heart. But they were the people I saw every day. They couldn't escape me—I was their cook. And I couldn't ignore them even though some of them scared me. I had to share with them the gospel that had brought me so much joy.

I tried to be friendly, and then casually mention that I was a Christian. I didn't want to force my ideas or "religion" on anyone. If someone said, "I don't want to talk about religion," I waited until he was ready.

When I was an atheist I had assumed that each person ought to make his or her own destiny because belief in God was pure wish fulfillment. It seemed to me atheism was "the only reasonable conclusion for a modern person based upon the facts of science." But my views had never been challenged in debate by an intelligent opponent.

As a new Christian and a young college student, I was eager to be that intelligent opponent for others who thought as I'd once thought. I didn't believe that it was reasonable to go through life without asking about its purpose and without considering whether life is controlled by impersonal fate or divine providence. I was convinced that if I shared the Christian faith in a rational and intelligent way, people would naturally want to know more about Jesus.

My first efforts, though, made me see that communicating the Christian faith is more than a matter of reasoning. Especially with the men at the boarding house, it was going to take more than a logical gospel presentation to bring Christ into their lives. I, the intellectual college student, had to learn to go where people really were. I found this out very quickly.

During my first two weeks in my new home, I mentioned in passing to a burly, bearded man that I was a Christian. He looked at me with contempt and rasped, "I am a member of the Socialist Labor Party, and we are as red as h—l." He then blasphemed against the Bible and said that he looked forward to the Red Revolution, the hour in history when all Christians would be placed against the wall—and eliminated.

The thought of my death seemed to give him pleasure.

Was he trying to scare the socks off of a twenty-year-old working in the kitchen? If that was what he had in mind, he succeeded. I did not want to give up on anyone. But this man said clearly that he hated me and all that I stood for. Reluctantly I decided that he was not open to the Christian message. I treated him courteously but for the time being didn't make any effort to tell him about Christ.

Then there was Tony. He was a tall, strong longshoreman. Was he made of the same stuff as this blasphemer? Possibly. While talking to me one day at breakfast, he said that he was an atheist. I just nodded and said that I used to be one, too. Should I try to talk to him about the Lord? He certainly did not look friendly. But after a time I decided that he was not like my red revolutionary. He spoke without bitterness when he said he was an atheist. So I tried to build a friendship with him.

The outward appearances were discouraging. Blond Tony in his black leather jacket looked like a cynical ex-soldier from a Hemingway novel. Occasionally he smiled, but most of the time he said little and ate dinner by himself, about three places away from the other boarders.

One evening, though, after eating, he pushed back his chair, peeled off his jacket, and said to the men sitting in the dining room, "Who'll arm wrestle me?"

He grinned as a couple of men headed for the door. The silence was deafening. After a few minutes I heard myself saying, "Tony, I'll wrestle you."

How in the world did I get myself into this predicament? As I settled into position and bent my arm, I knew my arm looked like a toothpick compared to his. I wondered if he could break or injure it. But I wanted to reach him for Christ, and I knew from my Oregon background that men like Tony respect courage. Maybe arm wrestling would build a bridge into his world that intellectual reasoning couldn't.

At any rate, in a moment our muscles were straining, our faces reddening. The strength of his arm was immense. What could I do but pray?

To his astonishment (and even more to mine), my arm did not move. He bent all his strength to the work, but my arm stayed where it was. A minute passed. He kept straining while my arm held like a rock.

I had no hope of putting down his arm. All I wanted to do was to keep my arm unmoved by his best effort. And that was exactly what happened. He could not move it!

Was there an angel in the dining room that night? Was Tony just being kind? He did not act like it. I felt him put all his strength into the battle. Maybe my arm had been strengthened by all the shoveling of sand and gravel I had done during my months on the highway crew.

Whatever the cause, my willingness to arm wrestle opened up Tony's life to me. Within a few days, we had the following conversation:

"Tony, you told me you were an atheist."

"Yeah, I don't believe in God. Religion's not for me."

"O.K., but let me ask you a question."

"Go ahead."

"Have you ever been really scared?"

"In North Africa I was. We were crossing an

open field, nobody around. Then the Stukas came. You know, the bombers that make the screaming noise? I tried to find a hole to hide. No holes, you tried to make one. No time, and the ground like rock. Then there was the howling of the Stukas and bombs hitting all around me. The ground was bouncing. Guys dead. It was h—l!"

For the first time I saw strong emotions in Tony. His cool exterior fell away, and we were there together feeling his fear.

I asked, "What did you do?"

He said, "I did what everybody else did. I prayed."

We then talked about his instinctive crying out to God in his fear, and he listened to my idea that he'd prayed because deep in his heart he knew that God existed.

In the weeks that followed, Tony and I talked more. From time to time I enlarged on my own testimony and tried to make the point that people are at war with God—which explained his present (and my past) atheism. Tony listened because he liked me, but communicating the gospel has several stages. Tony was at the first stage. He had come to respect a person with faith, and that was a major change for him.

But I needed to go deeper with Tony. Looking back now, I believe I was not courageous enough with him. I should have worked much harder (while praying) to reach his conscience. Tony did not understand himself very well. Like the rest of

us, he did not have a clue as to his real problem.
He needed to be faced, kindly and tenderly, with
his deepest motivations. My own wrestling with
the Bible had shown me that the real root of
atheism was a rebellion and hatred of God. Because I had his trust, I should have done more to
stand before Tony's heart's door and knock—
loudly. As an intellectual type, I was taking his
atheism too seriously. It wasn't his real problem.

Today I would talk to him frankly about the
sins that keep men back from Christ. Often sexual sins and the shame arising from them hinder
men from coming to Christ. They think, "Religion
is not for me." This really means, "There is no
way I could make myself worthy of God. Therefore why even make a stab at it?" Tony, I think,
had a completely wrong idea about Christ and
had no idea that the loving Lord has the power to
cleanse deep stains and dark memories. And because I was a new Christian myself, I also had
much to learn about the power of the gospel. If I
had taken this power more seriously, I would
have gone deeper in my conversations with Tony,
despite my fears and his resistance.

As a new Christian, I had the right idea in going to those closest to me with the gospel. Most new
Christians are surrounded with people who do not
believe in Christ as their Savior and Lord. Right
where we live and work, we have a wonderful opportunity to share what Jesus has done for us.

This was true for me at the boarding house. I

was in an unfamiliar setting. I had to depend on the people around me to learn how to do even the basics—cooking breakfast. I learned to enter into the rough-and-tumble world of a man like Tony. I learned to wait and let friendships develop.

This first stage is sometimes ignored by new Christians. Building friendships can be a slow, humbling process, when we do little more than wait and hope. In fact, we may be cast into the role of the "cook who can't cook," and need to lean on strangers to help us. This is not pleasant, but it builds relationships that are deep and caring.

The next stage is the one where we confront our new friends with the truth of the gospel. Waiting prepares us to confront the conscience and establishes our credibility as messengers of the cross. Now we must talk honestly with others about the wonderful reality of heaven and the dreadful reality of hell, and then insist that faith in Christ is the only way to experience the reality of heaven.

Some Christians want to rush in and confront others with the gospel without taking the time to build a relationship of trust. Others are wonderful at building relationships, but never take the next step and lovingly confront their friends with the claims of Christ. I have been guilty of both mistakes. This is when we learn what prayer is all about. As we pray, the Holy Spirit gives us what we need: the right combination of love and boldness as we share with others the words of life.

In San Francisco in 1948, there was a lot that I didn't know about sharing my faith. But the way God had changed me was fresh and new in my heart and mind. I wanted others to know about it and I intended to keep on sharing my new faith. I knew that sooner or later God would change others, too.

Faith up Close

San Francisco, 1949

"Why do you read the Bible all the time?" asked Mel.

"Mel, it's the only way I'm going to make it."

"Maybe I should read it too. What do you think?"

I didn't think Mel was serious. Unemployed, he was half drunk most of the time and hardly seemed in shape to read Romans with me. But I said, "Any time, Mel." I soon found out how literally Mel took my words.

One night around 1:00 A.M. he knocked several times on my door. I did not wake up. So he went to the end of the hall, made a mighty run at my door and slammed his way through it. Awake now and terrified, I saw a tall form swaying ominously over my bed. I leaped up and grappled desperately with my burglar.

Then I heard a familiar voice. "It's Mel! It's Mel! I . . . come to talk about religion . . . read the Bible."

"Mel," I said, shaking with agitation and disbelief, "you scared me to death." Calming down, I explained to him as best I could that he should come at some time other than the middle of the night. I then "helped"—which is to say half pushed—him out the door.

Mel's room in the boarding house was near mine, and he saw me studying my Bible all the time. I was convinced the only way I could survive was to go over and over the gospel message until it became the central focus of my life. At this point I was concentrating on Romans, and I pored over this book like a Bibleholic, until whole chapters were fixed in my memory. In the absence of my earthly father and brother I needed to hear the voice of my heavenly Father all the time.

It was this intensity of study that caught Mel's attention. He could see that we both had big needs, but I went to the Bible, while he went to the bottle. I think he sensed that I was getting life from my choice while he was getting death from his. When he asked to talk about religion, what he really wanted to know was whether what I was doing would help him—whether he, too, could get life from the Scriptures.

In the weeks that followed, I shared verses from Romans with him. We read them out loud from the Bible. Mel liked that, but he needed something more from me, because what he heard through his alcoholic haze did not satisfy his basic life thirst. He needed me to tell him *how* I received help from the Bible, and in a way that he could understand and identify with. I was just too green to see that. In my unconscious pride and ignorance, I was trying to educate him into salvation.

There is nothing wrong with giving a person the basic facts of the gospel message. After all, you cannot receive Christ without knowing who he is and what he has done. However, my approach was just too intellectual for Mel. It also omitted something totally basic. I did not tell him *how* I received powerful help from the Bible. Mel needed me to tell him how I became desperate and said, "Lord Jesus, I am terribly weak and sinful with a foolish mind, and I will die without your help!"

Mel could have understood that. He was close enough to me to see the effect of the gospel on my life, but I should have let him one step closer. I should have let him hear my words of confession and faith. I had allowed him into my Bible study life, but not my prayer life.

At this point in my Christian life, I was seeing my own need for the gospel more every day. The depth of need I felt did not unnerve me, because I was coming to understand that the gospel was *intended* for desperate people. My encounter with Mel helped me to see that others were as desperate as I was, and this combination of insights made me more confident in conversations about Christ and his work. People did not scare me as much—except, perhaps, when they burst into my room in the middle of the night!

Looking back, I can see how coming to Christ that afternoon in Oregon inevitably began to move me back in touch with people. This is God's way. I had returned to school, and as I settled in at the boarding house, I wanted to share how the gospel had changed my life with the other boarders. I often felt out of my depths with them, so far from the intellectual world of college. But this too I believe was God's design.

No doubt it's obvious by now that God had a way of bringing people into my life who were hard for me to care for or to talk with about the gospel. I had to face the fact that, by myself, I didn't love difficult people as God wanted me to. And by myself, I couldn't make the gospel clear to anyone—nice, intellectual, or otherwise.

Several weeks after Mel broke into my room, I had an encounter with a man who hated my cooking. Now, I thought my breakfast cooking had improved. But this man disagreed. Big John hated my breakfasts. He never thanked me; instead he enjoyed criticizing every move I made. Eggs were undercooked, toast was burnt, and the plate was cold. On and on he went, day after day. Sometimes it seemed he even blamed the windy, cold, San Francisco weather on me.

Then came a morning when it was too much. I blew up and told him what I thought of his complaining. Immediately I felt better, but later my conscience was troubled. I went to him and apologized, feeling that I had been a rotten example to Big John. But a strange look came over his face as if he had seen something for the first time.

He interrupted me, "Please, please, don't apologize. I think you are right. All my life I have been a complainer. And you are right—I'm not thankful for anything. I'm so ashamed."

It was as if I had lanced a boil. More confessions followed, messy, but wonderfully healing. Afterwards, he asked me what to do, speaking softly with genuine sorrow. On my part I was having trouble processing all this. Was this man thanking me for my outburst? Most people instinctively defend themselves when criticized; he was just the opposite. Where was the man who enjoyed being mean to me every morning? Was my bitter breakfast critic asking me for help? The change was so abrupt and so profound that I wondered, "Is this some kind of new game he's playing?"

I didn't know what to do, but I could see that the Lord wanted me to get closer to John. John had humbled himself by accepting my criticism. I now had to humble myself, forgive, and become his friend. I did not like John, and I did not want to get closer to him, but God intervened. His grace touched my heart.

I heard myself saying, "Let's get together after breakfast." He responded with enthusiasm.

I fed the last man and washed the dishes slowly. I wasn't looking forward to more time with Big John. He had been criticizing me without let-up for several weeks, and I had a good recollection of all the bad stuff he had said. But I knew God wanted me to accept him as a friend. So that morning I studied Romans with him. He was as open and willing as a child. That afternoon, after a further talk about Christ's work on the cross, we knelt in his bedroom and he prayed to receive Christ.

Now I was really amazed. Was this change for real? It was a revolution in one day in a twisted human life. I had forgotten that the same thing had happened to me about five months earlier even more quickly, in a single afternoon.

Soon afterwards I asked my pastor, Carl Ahlfeldt, to visit John. I still had my doubts, but Carl reported that the man seemed genuinely changed by God. John was now my friend, and he soon came to church. But the real proof to me of his change of heart was the way he began thanking me for breakfast!

A couple of weeks later he became seriously ill. Let it be said that it had nothing to do with my breakfasts. When I went to the hospital to see him, I found him full of joy. Carl visited him too, and he reported that John was contented and full of faith. Then Barbara McKenzie, a Christian nurse in the hospital and a good friend of mine, began visiting him to share the Bible with him and pray. He grew quickly in Christ as he was brought within the circle of a believing community.

My breakfast critic had now become my friend. I didn't really feel as if I had done anything. I had simply lived my life of faith next to him, cooking breakfast and trying (at first unsuccessfully) to be his friend. But it hadn't stopped there. As we lived in close proximity, I could see what his sin patterns were and then confront him. I will be the first to say that I did this partly out of concern for myself—not for him! But the Holy Spirit was the one who was really active in John's life. I was just his (at times unwitting and unwilling) instrument. When I told John how his sins affected me, his conscience was reached. He wanted to confess his sins and be forgiven. That was not me. That was the Holy Spirit.

I was watching God do some interesting things. Neither Mel nor John was religious. But they weren't prejudiced against Christ; they didn't freeze into silence at the name of Jesus. They were both prepared by God's working under the surface of their lives. They both had some sense of need that was compelling: Mel, with his alcohol problem, and Big John, with his bitter complaining. This sense of need and their willingness to admit it were God's work. He opened both of them up to listen to the message of the cross.

The Holy Spirit is the one who is always working behind the scenes. His method is always successful, and we can be confident that in every situation he is triumphant. The message of the cross as applied by the Spirit saves souls. Nothing else can do it, but the cross can break the hardest heart. It broke mine. It broke John's. This is the humbling strategy of a sovereign God.

At twenty I didn't understand everything in this chapter. Far from it. But I was learning more about sharing Christ by living in this boarding house and cooking breakfast than I ever could have learned from a systematic course of instruction.

I was learning to let others into my life. Mel could see me studying the Bible and finding something there that changed and satisfied me. That's why he wanted to study the Bible, too. And I lived close enough to John to be fed up with his sins—and to let him know (less than perfectly) how they affected me. There at the boarding house, the men could see that I had the same sins and needs as they did and that my God helped me. The Holy Spirit did the rest.

So wherever you "cook breakfast," there is your classroom for learning to share your faith. The people you encounter daily are the ones Jesus wants you to share the gospel with. But make sure that you are understanding and loving the gospel more each day yourself or you will not be able to love and understand the friends at your "breakfast table."

Faith and Two Kinds of Truth

CHAPTER THREE

San Francisco, 1948–49

Drink was not the only passion at the boarding house. Some of us also had a passion for the truth. Gus was my fellow student at San Francisco State and my cooking coach. He liked to fight for what he believed to be true. So did I. But our definitions of truth were diametrically different.

One night during my first month on Eddy Street, Gus and I were sitting in his room, talking about God's existence. He made it clear that he did not believe in God at all and that he had trouble understanding how any reasonable human being could believe in God in the light of modern science.

Our conversation grew more heated when I said that his confidence in Charles Darwin was akin to a religious faith. "The facts," I argued, "are all against Darwin."

I insisted Darwin's theory of the descent of

the species was "simply unprovable, and there was a great deal of evidence against it." Gus's view was that biology gave Darwin total support, and reasonable people should be able to see it. He was a biology student and knew a lot more about the subject than I did, but that didn't stop me, and we went on arguing for hours.

Gus was a friendly, pleasant person who smiled readily. He was not a natural shouter in conversation, and neither was I. But we both cared a great deal about the truth, even though we disagreed about its content. We cared so much that the hours slipped away as we went at each other with angry voices.

Later, we cooled off. But we remained appalled at the other's inability to see and accept the truth. At the beginning our conversations seemed fruitless and discouraging. But we kept at it and our friendship was not destroyed by our arguments. Actually, we both enjoyed them. Gus was Bill's assistant in preparing the evening meal for the boarders. Afterwards we often would go to Gus's room and talk until late.

We had much in common. We lived and worked together and were students in the same school. And we were "modern" people in the way that philosophers use the term: we had both started out in adult life believing that human reason alone could discover the truth about the world and human nature. But I lost my faith in reason's ability to provide ultimate answers. After my encounter with God in Oregon, the Bible had become my basis for understanding life and the world.

Nevertheless, Gus and I were alike in that neither of us was a relativist. We both believed that truth is something objective, something that is "out there" to be discovered. We both believed that truth mattered and had to be taken into account when you lived your life. It was this common passion for truth that led to our heated exchanges.

The chasm between us existed because we differed on where that truth can be found. Gus's hope was in human reason, the "modern" outlook influenced by the eighteenth-century Enlightenment. My hope was the Bible and the tradition of historic Christianity.

Bill, the owner of the boarding house, stood in contrast to Gus as a man before his time. To him, nothing was really fixed and objectively true. It just depended on your point of view. He was a *postmodern* person, even though he was much older than either of us. By *postmodern* I mean anyone who sees life through his wish list and emotions. If that seems too strong, you can say that the postmodernist believes that truth is different things for different people. Truth is a matter of preference, not of unalterable reality.

Bill also had an idealistic hope that "things would work out," but his hope had little basis in fact. His hope was in his own creative powers. He liked the idea that "you can re-invent yourself if necessary."

His business was just such an invention, an unreal cardboard dream.

Soon after I began to live in his boarding house, I went into Bill's living room and unexpectedly saw why he limped so heavily. His lower legs were exposed and he was putting ointment on them. They were ghastly, with skin eroded away and naked, infected flesh exposed over a wide area on both legs.

Seeing the concern on my face, he said, "I know I should be in the hospital, and some day I'll go in and get these legs treated, but not now. I need to make this place a success first."

The contradiction between reality and his plans did not seem to bother him, but it did me. To make this place succeed he needed a healthy body and legs. It took a lot of walking and working to make it go. But the more he walked and worked, the worse Bill's legs would become, and the less successful would be the running of his business.

Like many *postmoderns*, Bill also had a weak moral center. I soon found out that deceit and lying were a way of life to him.

During the first week I came to live there I told Bill about my conversion, and he nodded respectfully. I had told him, "I was a student here but I dropped out because I was confused about myself and life. I went back home to Oregon. I guess I expected the beautiful natural world to heal me. Instead, the longer I stayed the more confused I became, so I started to read the Bible.

"I did not get much out of it until one day I read that God wanted me to live for him all the way. I suddenly realized that I did not know how to live for God. I lived exclusively for myself. It hit me like a rock in the face that I was a totally egocentric person who always thought first about old number one.

"I asked God to forgive me, and he did. Jesus gave me a peace of mind so beautiful that words can't really describe it."

Bill did not seem hostile to what I had said. It was an interesting point of view. But it did not dent him.

Shortly afterwards he began to ask me to deliver sealed envelopes to "Mabel" who ran a bakery on Fillmore Street. I did so willingly because of his inability to walk distances. But it did not take long before this naive twenty year old figured out that he was being used as a runner to place illegal bets on the horses.

I was shocked at being used in this way. I had talked to Bill from the heart about what Christ meant to me, and in response, he deceived me into doing something that was contrary to my beliefs and exposed me to possible arrest.

Once I concluded that Mabel was a bookie, I said to Bill, "We need to talk, Bill, about those envelopes. Are you using me to place illegal bets?"

He nodded. I then asked, "And you did it knowing that I am a Christian?"

He laughed and said that he knew I would eventually understand what was happening and refuse to do it any longer. But I pressed him just a bit more. I asked, "Did you think about what you were doing? Did you understand that if the bakery was raided I would be arrested and have a police record?"

He did not reply, shrugging it off by saying he could get someone else to act as his runner. From then on, I became more cautious about Bill, convinced that there was a self-centered twist in him that made it impossible for him and me to communicate.

But my conversations with Gus continued, quieter now. On New Year's Eve, 1948, I invited him to come with me to a young people's gathering in our church. He told me, "I'll come for a while, but I'll leave before midnight for Market Street." This was the place where the New Year's action would take place and Gus wanted to be there.

To his surprise, he thoroughly enjoyed meeting the friendly young people at our church and soon was playing games and laughing with the rest of us. Then around 11:00 P.M.—the time he was to leave—the group began to talk about what Jesus meant to them. Gus did not move; he just listened. Shortly before midnight we all began to pray one by one with much joy. I don't recall the time of our departure, but as Gus and I walked down the street, he said, in words that electrified me, "I don't see how anyone could be here tonight and come away an atheist."

Gus was no longer an atheist! I had let him into my life, but that hadn't changed him. But when I brought him into the community of faith, he saw something that he'd never seen before. He saw that our faith gave us love for each other—and that was something new and attractive. It wasn't just the fun we had; it was the way we cared for each other.

Gus was attracted by the warmth and acceptance of Christians, and he was moved by their prayers. He saw something more real— something he hadn't found in biology class. So I invited him to a prayer meeting! We walked together the mile or more to the Wednesday evening service at our church building on Turk Street.

The "prayer meeting" was really more of a Bible study led by the pastor, but Gus liked it, and began to talk seriously about the basis of Christian belief. Our discussions together now concerned the content and teaching of the Bible. Gus always seemed to have an endless supply of questions.

Later that spring I asked Gus, "When are you going to become a Christian?" The question came partly out of concern for him and partly out of impatience.

He paused and said simply, "I think I have."

"You have become a Christian?!"

"Yes," he said, with a wide smile.

I was delighted and humbled by the grace my Father had given my friend. Gus was best man at my wedding a year later and, over the years, the one friend from the boarding house I've stayed in contact with. He married and worked as a businessman in California.

Not long after Gus's conversion, our boarding house closed down because Bill's legs forced him to enter a Veteran's hospital. During the last few days of May, Gus and I worked for Bill, cleaning and washing up the place. Gus and I had been cooking partners and intellectual sparring partners. Now we were partners in caring for Bill after everyone else had left him. Gus had seen people love and care for one another at our church. Now together, Gus and I were bringing that into Bill's house.

On the last day, I was cleaning his room when Bill said, "I have underestimated you."

I stopped my cleaning and looked at him closely.

He continued, "There were others I thought were my friends. They forgot about me when things came out this way. But you and Gus stuck with me and worked to the end."

I don't remember what was said next. What stayed in my mind was his belated appreciation. It took me completely by surprise and left me speechless. Looking back now, I can see that it was at least a partial apology.

Bill knew what I believed and had shown no interest in it. He had used Gus and me in many small ways, and thought nothing of it. But possibly there was something important here that I could have done.

Bill's moment of truth had come. He was now alone, very much alone. The hard fact was that his life was in danger from the disease in his legs. At the very best, he would need to spend many months in the VA hospital. He was now vulnerable, and maybe humbled. At this moment he might have listened to me. Today I think I would have offered to pray for him. The decision to accept prayer would have been his. I would not have tried to put any pressure on him in his weakened state. Regrettably, the thought did not occur to me at the time. I had assumed he was a closed person. Perhaps he was, but I never found out by completing our final conversation.

Here is what I might have said. "Bill, I want to thank you for the job and for putting up with my efforts to cook breakfasts. I'm really sorry to see you go into the hospital. I know this must be very hard for you. Would you be willing to let me pray for you?"

But I did not say those words, so I do not know what his answer might have been. If he had asked for prayer, I would have asked if he would accept a hospital visit from our pastor.

But I did not give Bill the option. I had such reservations about him in my mind that I was just not ready to move into his life. My apprenticeship in life was far from complete. I had a lot to learn.

A few days after the boarding house closed, Gus drove me to my home town in Gold Beach, Oregon. After a few weeks I found a job working in the forest service for the summer, where I, God's beginner, continued to move forward, having a lot of fun, albeit with a certain amount of stumbling on the road.

In six months' time the Holy Spirit had renewed the lives of at least three highly resistant people, beginning with me, then Big John, and finally Gus. Though my part in it was flawed, God did use my faith in Christ to bring these two others to faith. He also used the house on Eddy Street to build my confidence in my Father's power to work in people's hearts.

Many Christians fail to share their faith because they are trying to do it perfectly, and since they cannot do it perfectly, they remain silent. But what we learn from my story is that God is pleased to use imperfect people like me.

What really convinces others of the truth of the Christian message is not our perfection or our rational arguments, but our willingness to love them where they are and to introduce them to our community of faith. God does not want us to share our faith as independent supermen or

superwomen, but as brothers and sisters together in God's family. Gus, the modern man,
was changed by his contact with this community. After he became a part of it, we were able to
surprise our postmodern boss with the love of
the body of Christ.

Sharing My Faith with the "Virtuous"

CHAPTER FOUR

Oregon, 1949

I liked most of the men in the boarding house on Eddy Street, and now that it was closed, I would miss them. But I don't think any of them—with the possible exception of Bill—would have called themselves "virtuous." And no one else would have, either.

As Gus and I drove north on Highway 101, I knew I was headed home to the traditional Oregon of 1949, where many of the people I knew *would* count themselves among the virtuous. I looked forward to being with them. They were my people, and I knew them well.

Concepts like modern and postmodern were laughable to them. They were more interested in the natural world than in the world of ideas. Instead of arguing about how the world began, they told stories about the natural world itself. They loved to talk about their hunting and fishing exploits and the funny things they saw their animals do. They were good neighbors and would never have dreamed of involving me in numbers running, as Bill did. They tried to live by a moral code that was based on good stuff—honesty, kindness, and keeping your word—and the duty to work hard and pay your bills.

Some of them went to church, but most did not. But although they were not churchgoers, they had moral standards derived from the teachings of the Bible.

One night on our trip north, Gus and I camped after dark beside the Eel River. After a snack we spread our blankets on the ground in a redwood grove in a deep valley. As I prepared to sleep, I looked up at the stars massed overhead. The view was overwhelming. For months I had lived in San Francisco, where the stars, obscured by the city lights, hardly seemed to come out at night. But here in this valley among the redwoods all was dark, with not a hint of light, and the majesty of the night sky was absolutely commanding. Looking at that concentrated glory, I worshiped the God of all creation, who made those perfect heavens and the magnificent redwood forest.

At that moment I felt my finitude and his splendid infinity, and was comforted and exalted at the same time. I was happy to be his creature and his child. The God who made all this was with me. He had sent his Son to die for me, and his Spirit to change me. He was with me. I was now falling in love with a young woman in San Francisco, but I had already fallen in love with God my Father. This awareness prepared me for the days that were to come. Any struggles I might have while following him seemed like nothing compared to the pleasure I had in knowing God.

The next day Gus and I arrived in Gold Beach, and after another day he headed back to California. I was back home and it felt good. I began to look for a job.

During those first days home, I also talked with my mother to tell her more about what happened to me the previous fall. Right after my conversion I had talked to her about Christianity in a different way. I told her that I knew God and that I had joy and peace. She had been puzzled.

Now that I was home for the summer, I brought the subject up again. I think my mother understood the words I was saying, but she really came from a different world. I was once again talking about "joy" while she looked puzzled. For her, being a Christian meant going to church and believing in the Bible. But most of all it meant being moral, kind, and generous.

But joy? Peace with God? Wanting to tell everybody about Jesus? Well, maybe. But somehow it did not seem to connect. And I became painfully aware how hard it is for virtuous people to see how much they need God.

My mother really was a virtuous person. She had endured the hardships of homesteading, rearing eight children, early widowhood, and a troubled second marriage. But I had never heard her complain, an unusual quality in anybody. Unwilling to gossip, she was kind to her friends and neighbors and prepared to make every sacrifice for her family.

Not only was she kind to people, but she also loved animals, especially dogs and horses. Her father (and my grandfather), Thomas Murray, had owned a horse ranch in Salinas, California, and respect and loving care for animals was part of her very being. She functioned with a moral code that made her dependable and easy to get along with, and she had a self-discipline that was awesome.

I had figured out how to talk to the men in the boarding house in San Francisco. It was easy to see how much they needed help. But this was my mother. I was timid, almost diffident.

Still, I plunged in. "Mom, I'm wondering. You know we all grew up thinking we were Christians, went to church, and all that. But I can't recall anyone ever telling me that I was lost and that I needed Jesus to give me a new life."

She replied, "Of course, I always believed that." She said, "We (meaning herself and my father) took it for granted."

I stopped, feeling confused. I wanted to respect her, but I was troubled by the thought that Christ and his love was a thing "we took for granted." She left me completely puzzled, because during the years I had known her, she had never said anything like, "Christ died for our sins, and it means everything to me." Why the silence? Was it simply a generational difference?

I asked more questions, but each time she agreed completely with my concerns. What do you do with that? According to her she had accepted these things privately. She did not know that she "had never talked about them to us as children." She thought she had.

I remembered her strongly emphasizing the Ten Commandments and the Lord's second coming. She taught us about Christ's return as a way to keep us in line. None of us wanted to be caught breaking one of the commandments when Jesus reappeared! In fact, I got into the habit of always looking to the east before I did anything wrong. I figured that if I didn't see a cloud in the east, I was safe.

What I learned from my mother was the law, but not a relationship with the lawgiver and forgiver. Growing up I expected that only the good guys were going to make it through the Judgment Day. I didn't think there was much chance for me, since as a youngster I did not like Jesus. I was especially disappointed by his strange teaching that you should turn the other cheek when wronged.

But now I loved Jesus and those "strange" teachings had changed my life. I wanted to share with my mother the joy I had in knowing Christ, and the relief I felt. There was no longer a part of me searching the sky for the coming judge. Instead, I knew that I was forgiven for the many times I had broken the law my parents had taught me. And I had a heavenly Father to replace the earthly father and brother I missed so much.

I had a hard time expressing all this to my mother, so I just kept trying to share with her the joy I now had in my life.

My next conversation with a virtuous relative proved even more frustrating. It was 1949 and jobs were scarce. While I was looking for one, I met my cousin Reid and his wife Mary at the street corner near our house. They were going through the neighborhood taking orders for vegetables and fruits. Once Reid saw me, his blue eyes sparkled and a smile spread all over his face. Soon Reid and Mary were handing me choice fruits to sample, and they were telling me all about their prosperous farm.

Reid said with approval, "I hear you have become religious. Now, Mary and I never go to church, but we are glad you do. Keep it up, Jack. But you know us—we just live by the golden rule, doing to others what we'd want them to do to us. It works; we're really happy people."

All the time he was talking, he was handing me fruit, and I accepted with gratitude. It was of excellent quality. Finally, he asked me something about what I believed, but before I could answer, he interrupted by telling me some of the ways he and Marie kept the "golden rule."

I heard a lot about the "golden rule" from Reid as I stood with him on that street corner. He was really convinced that he had an outstanding moral character and that anyone else could have one too with a little practical effort. Then, just as I began to ask a question about his beliefs, a neighbor two blocks down the street waved at them, and Reid shouted something like, "Sorry, Jack. I've got to deliver food." Mary and Reid jumped into their van and were gone.

I was left standing there with my mouth open and my hands full of beautiful fruit. But I was puzzled and maybe a little amused. Could anybody, I asked myself, be that good? Strike two for sharing my faith with the virtuous.

After a time I obtained a job in the forest service on an isolated mountain lookout about nine miles from the coast, and here I once again encountered the work of the virtuous. After a few days a cowboy showed up at my door, climbed down from his horse, and handed me some food, explaining that it must get lonesome in this high and lonely spot. He thought maybe a little fresh food might be appreciated.

I immediately recognized his smiling face and greeted him warmly. I had known Gary since I was a child. When I was a boy, he had let me drive his truck! A very exciting thing for a nine year old.

Over lunch he told me that he had dug out my leaf-filled spring, and that should make it easier for me to get my water each evening. Again I was grateful, and now I was convinced that I was being haunted by the legion of the good guys.

As we drank our coffee, he began to tell me about a religious experience he'd had recently. He had become very sick, arriving at the hospital near death's door, and he had prayed with confident trust in God, with the result that he had an astonishing healing. He never went to church, but he said, "The big outdoors is my church."

This time I was determined at least to say *something,* and say it quickly before he packed up his virtues and departed in haste. So I told him how God had changed my twisted life, and how the cause of the twist had been "my fists fighting against God." I then gave him some examples of things in my life that the Lord had changed.

I seemed to connect with him, but soon he remembered that God and he were already doing just fine together. So I took out my Bible and we read together the Ten Commandments. I went over the key ones that set forth obvious sins like hatred, jealousy, sexual lust, adultery, and impure hearts.

Would he leave now? No, he stayed for at least two hours, and we went over the way to come to Christ as set forth in Romans. I sprin-

kled my explanation of the Bible with personal il-
lustrations. Friendly to the last, he went his way,
at least outwardly convinced that he was not a
sinner, trusting that the God of the great outdoors would accept him on the basis of his good
works.

As I thought about these conversations, I
started to understand those who are convinced
of their almost-perfect goodness. In some ways
they are the opposite of the men at the boarding
house.

They are usually private people, self-contained,
and, on the inside, lonely. I learned that their willingness to confide and be open with me was actually a compliment. I was being trusted.

But their virtues had hidden vices that they
themselves could not see, at least not with any
clarity. The "virtuous" are often irritable and im-
patient perfectionists; control freaks who judge
harshly and hastily, blaming and accusing others when things go wrong. They would never let
themselves be consumed by drink, but they
could be consumed by their own accomplishments. All these things are rooted in deep pride.

For years I struggled with how to share my
faith with the virtuous. My point of breakthrough
came when I eventually discovered that I was one
of these "perfect people" myself. Everything I dis-
liked about the "virtuous," especially their arrogance and controlling spirit, were the hallmarks
of my own life.

After seeing this, I talked with my mother again, but I now had a heart attitude she could understand. God himself, I believe, had timed the visit. A few months earlier, my mother had experienced a terrible conflict with a relative who had deeply hurt her just when she was recovering from a major heart attack.

I took my mother to lunch, and over coffee I talked to her about myself. I wanted her to see me as a sinner, critical of others while feeling superior to them. I wanted her to see me as I had come to see myself—a sinner who needed grace.

I then asked her if she had ever considered the idea that our family majored in pride, which displayed itself in our feeling superior to other people. I wondered aloud, "Am I the only sinner in the crowd?"

Then I told her what I was like on the inside: "I was proud, self-righteous, and judgmental, hateful and hating. And if left to myself, I am still going to act this way. Only Christ's death on my behalf can cleanse me and keep on cleansing me. I'm in desperate need of his grace every day."

Mother looked thoughtful and didn't answer. I continued, telling her how pride had expressed itself in my life, affecting those I loved in destructive ways.

Finally she agreed that "we are a proud family." We talked about what that meant, and she made it clear that she really understood what was being said. I tried to ask with all tenderness,

"Do you remember your deep disappointment with the relative who treated you so selfishly recently?"

Her sorrow was now seen in her face. We were silent, so that she could have time to digest what I was saying.

I said, "Look, Mom, I didn't exploit you that way, but I have the same kind of hard heart by nature. We all do. Without Christ's constant help, I am naturally just like that. We all have deep-down evil in ourselves, and it reveals itself in selfish behavior and self-righteous attitudes. That's why we all so desperately need the cross of Christ."

I believe that, for the first time, I was able to help my mother see why the cross is necessary for us "good people." Underneath it all, I was saying, our sins may be worse than those of the lawless types we feel superior to. There was a oneness between us that day that meant a great deal to me and, I believe, to her.

After this conversation, my sister and I noticed a change in my mother. We believe that it was then that she understood for the first time that she was a sinner who needed a Savior. Our conversation did not end there; we continued to talk about it over the years that followed. Now we could talk much more honestly, and we were able to bring other family members into this new dialogue.

From this conversation with my mother, I learned that I didn't need to attack "virtuous people" to show them that I was more virtuous than they. Instead, they needed to hear about my sins and weaknesses first of all. I needed to open up my life and my heart to them, just as I had to the people in the boarding house. When I shared with them how God had broken me and how he was cleansing me from my vices and virtues, then I saw God work.

Camping in the redwoods had given me a glimpse of the glory of God in the heavens, and over the years I saw that same power displayed in my own family. It was that power, the power to create and the power to change hard hearts, that gave me confidence as I went back to school in the fall.

Facing the Skeptics

CHAPTER FIVE

San Francisco, 1950

"Mr. Fox," said the professor, "you are a Christian. You believe in the Bible, don't you?"

"Yes, I do," answered Mr. Fox.

"And you believe that the world is ruled by laws that make possible an orderly universe?"

"Yes."

Dr. Trask pressed his point, "Then how can you believe in miracles if the world is governed by laws of cause and effect? Mr. Fox, Mr. Fox, are you thinking clearly? How can the cosmos be orderly if miracles are constantly interrupting its structure?"

"I don't know," said Mr. Fox. Confusion was written all over his face. The questioning went on and on, and you could see that Dr. Thomas Trask, head of the philosophy department and the lion of San Francisco State, had just eaten another fundamentalist lamb.

Friends had warned me about Dr. Trask.

"He's a religious modernist, and he's attacked and undermined the faith of many a would-be Christian."

Next week was my turn. "Mr. Miller," he began, "you believe that God made the world, don't you?"

I nodded. And the lion moved closer to another poor, edgy lamb. He continued, all politeness, "You know that the engineers who put up the Golden Gate Bridge built it depending on the unchangeable laws of nature. I refer to laws established by the Creator."

I leaned heavily on the Lord and gathered my courage. I said to him, "I'm not quite sure I understand what you are saying."

He smiled, and now I was really scared. I felt strangely alone in the large, crowded classroom.

"I'm asking, how can you believe that the Golden Gate Bridge will continue to stand unless the laws of nature cannot be interrupted by miracles? How can we build anything unless the laws of cause and effect govern the world? How can you believe in miracles that break the laws of an orderly universe?"

My fear began to fade. I said slowly, "I still don't think I understand your definition of 'the laws of nature.' When you say 'laws' what do you mean?" He suddenly turned benign and walked around the room. He then said that God cannot break his own laws and be trustworthy; therefore there is no place for miracles if God is dependable.

I then said, "I think you are assuming we agree on the definition of 'the laws of the universe.' Probably we disagree. From my point of view it's the plan of God that makes the Golden Gate Bridge stand, not an unbreakable chain of natural laws. Both laws and miracles are included in God's orderly plan. So I don't see any conflict between laws and miracles."

When he heard my words, "plan of God," he looked at me for a moment, unexpectedly silent. At the time I was not sure why these words gave him pause. I thought that he was intrigued to discover someone who believed in the sovereignty of God—a God whose grand plan controls all of the world and its history. He took up the next class card and said, "Mr. Fraley, tell me what you think about. . . ."

The doctrine of God's sovereignty was one that I had struggled with when I first became a Christian, but as I read my Bible, I found it everywhere I looked. Eventually this teaching became a great comfort to me as I understood that God's wise control was over every part of life, both the miraculous and the ordinary. What I said in class was almost a direct quotation from J. Gresham Machen's book *A Christian View of Man*. I learned later that Dr. Trask recognized this Christian philosopher's influence on me.

It was this dependence on God's plan that led me to take a bold step. If God really had "the whole world in his hands," I had no need to fear

Dr. Trask. So sometime within the next month I went to see Trask in his office. After sitting down, I told him that I had been an atheist who had been changed by Christ.

I began to explain to him the story of that change. I told him that reading Machen's book had initially made me furious. I couldn't understand—and didn't like—the idea of God being in charge of every part of my life. It deeply offended my sense of independence, fostered by my Oregon upbringing and many years of fending for myself. If there was one thing I had learned from my family, it was the importance of self-reliance. Until I met Christ, this had been my religion.

I told Dr. Trask, "After reading Machen I immediately turned to the Bible to see if what he wrote was in there. When I came to Ephesians 1, I discovered that it was. This chapter exposed my deep pride and turned me into different person."

I forgot that this was my professor and said, "God showed me my ugly egocentricity, and this knowledge of my deep sinfulness drove me to trust in Christ's work on the cross for me. My surrender to Jesus has given me a joy that I can't find words to express."

Then I came to the hard part. I believe that the Spirit prompted me to say, "Dr. Trask, I'm troubled by what you did to Mr. Fox. He came to your class a believer and will leave it deeply confused. He is a simple person and untaught. I don't think what you did to him was right." I did not quote Scripture, but I had in mind Christ's severe warning about people who cause his little ones to stumble (Matthew 18:1–14).

Dr. Trask defended himself without acting like the brilliant showman of the classroom. That was a relief. He said that faith is not worth anything unless it is tested by tough questioning. He then astonished me by opening up his life to me in the same way that I had with him. He talked at length about his own journey as a graduate student and as a minister in a mainline Protestant denomination. I had the same church background myself.

Then he grew confessional and said that he had studied under J. Gresham Machen at Princeton Theological Seminary. But later he had become skeptical about God's sovereignty, and Christ's atonement, bodily resurrection, and second coming, and finally he had written J. Gresham Machen to tell him about his move into liberal theology.

His words were unforgettable. "Machen wrote only a brief note to acknowledge my long letter. He did not say much more than that 'I would understand when I became older.' I was disappointed."

Suddenly my heart was stirred with compassion. "Dr. Trask," I heard myself saying, "come to faith. There is no other hope for a sinner like me except Jesus and his blood, and that hope can be yours." My heart went out to him. I felt he was throwing away his eternal hope for the sake of a human philosophy that was already going out of style.

I walked out of his office sorrowing over his refusal to surrender to Christ. Then I realized that I had just presented the gospel to a modernist philosopher and theologian. It was the Holy Spirit who prompted me to love him instead of being intimidated by him. And it was the Spirit that had spoken as I urged him to believe the message of the cross and put his trust in a risen, living Christ.

I left my professor, saddened by his superficial skepticism. I wanted him to see that his doubts did not go deep enough. I believed that doubts about the powers of human reason were healthy and right. I had learned to doubt everything, including my own faith in human reason, and this doubting had led me to faith in Christ.

With my thinking stimulated by this conflict, I resolved to witness as *God's* skeptic to a world where people like Trask were believing when they should be skeptical. He had his faith entirely in the wrong place. He was trusting reason as his final authority, making his human mind into his Bible.

I believe in God's sovereign plan. I believe it holds the world together (both laws and miracles) and gives it a destiny. I believe that my encounter with Trask was part of that plan. Who but a naive student would tell this prominent scholar and churchman that he needed to become more skeptical about his faith in human reason? Who but someone led by the Spirit would, like a childlike friend, ask this famous man to surrender his life to Christ?

For this young college student to confront a full professor with his need for forgiveness in Jesus—it was exhilarating! I could have been tempted to congratulate myself, but my Father made sure that I kept growing in real dependence on him instead of just talking about it. He used the manual labor jobs that I took to support myself to keep me in the real world.

The boarding house was closed, but my cooking lessons there stood me in good stead. I got a job as student manager of the college cafeteria. There I met Gracie, an African-American woman who worked in the dishwashing room. In the years since, I have often thought of her as one of my best teachers and mentors.

I loved Gracie, and so did everyone else. But Gracie had high standards and there was one thing she would not tolerate: bad manners.

Some days the cafeteria was jam-packed with students. The tables would be overflowing with dishes. Naturally, on those days, I forgot everything else to rush to the rescue when I came to work around noon. But Gracie would not have that. No matter how overwhelmed I was with work, I was to enter the dishwashing room with a warm smile and a clear greeting—no matter what the dining room chaos. If I forgot, she thundered, "White boy! White boy!" Nothing could happen until I stopped and apologized.

I wasn't allowed to rush away after the greeting, either. I had to stop for a little chat—not long, but enough to show her that I cared and respected her.

Sometimes on rainy, chaotic days I would forget, and then Gracie shouted at me. To receive her forgiveness (and stop the shouting) I would have to reenact the scene and do it right. In front of the crowded dining room and amid the jobs waiting to be done, I would walk away and then turn around and make a new entrance with perfect manners—to the delight of Gracie and any staff on hand.

Gracie was part of God's training for me. Who but beloved Gracie would beat into my young, impetuous head the importance of taking time to show respect for people? Would the skeptics like Dr. Trask have listened if I hadn't learned to share my faith with a respect and consideration for others—even in greeting and conversation?

A few months later I got another part-time job working for the post office at Rincon Annex, along with about two hundred other San Francisco State students. Since much of the work there was routine, we had time to talk. My questions for other people were becoming more penetrating, and because of Gracie's training, I now knew how important it was to have good manners and a welcoming demeanor.

The best conversations usually took place when another student and I worked alone. Trading information about academic studies and interests would often lead to talk about more serious concerns. Most of them said they didn't have any religious belief, but they usually had some kind of secular faith. Biology majors would want to talk about evolution. I would challenge their evolutionary theory and talk about the claims of the Creator. History majors would maintain a belief in human progress, but it wasn't too hard to convince them that there was evil inside the human heart.

Psychology majors would want to talk about fear and guilt. They would tell me how Freud had solved the guilt problem by labeling it the by-product of father-child conflict. I would then challenge their assumption that the guilt was not real. I asked how Freud knew for sure that guilt came from conflicts between fathers and sons. Though that may happen, doesn't it take a lot of faith to believe that the human conscience was created by family conflicts?

I had recently married Rose Marie Carlsen, a friend from church. Our experiences in learning how to be married gave me plenty of examples I could use to talk about my real guilt.

"Forget about 'faith' for a moment," I would say. "Look at the obvious fact: when I do something wrong, my conscience tells me flat out 'you did something really bad.' Sometimes I get selfish and demanding with Rose Marie, and when she tells me about it, I can't say that this is 'neurosis.' My conscience tells me I'm guilty, and the fact is I am!" Such a conversation would often lead into a presentation of why Christ's death on the cross was the only cure for human guilt and the fear of death.

One evening it was very clear that God had orchestrated the whole encounter between me and my coworker for the night. I was working on the mezzanine where the mail bags were emptied. Larger items were removed along with special delivery letters, and the rest were dumped down chutes to sorting tables on the floor below. Once my work was all caught up, I moved back to chat with a new coworker, a student named Bob.

He also had finished his work and together we were waiting for more mail bags. By now my reputation as a Christian was rather widespread, and he asked me about my beliefs. I told him a little about myself, but not much. I then waited for him to say something. Smiling, he expressed some hesitant doubts about the Bible, as in, "Just suppose some of it is not true?"

I grinned, and said something like, "But maybe you should doubt your doubts?"

He explained that he did not mean to be disrespectful, but he wondered how you could tell whether the Bible was true. I replied, "Every page shows the touch of God. Read it and you will see it. It's full of Christ, and Christ compels real believing."

He looked very serious at that moment and said, "I *have* been reading it, with my wife Pauline."

"You have?"

"Yes," he explained. "We have been reading it with a Jehovah's Witness, and we have questions that we'd like to talk over with someone who knows the Bible. We're hungry for help."

From time to time throughout the evening, Bob and I chatted about the Bible. He pressed me with questions. After work we talked freely for a longer time, and he told an amazing story.

"Last night," he said, "Pauline and I got down on our knees and prayed. We even said we were willing to sell Watchtowers on the street corner if this teaching were true. We were very serious, knowing we had to come to a decision. We asked God to show us what was true. And then tonight I meet you!"

We kept talking each night, and soon Bob and Pauline attended an evangelistic series held in our church. They both gave their lives to Christ in childlike faith.

What made the difference between Dr. Trask and Bob and Pauline? Certainly, they all heard the message. All of them had heard Jesus lovingly command sinners to come to himself

(Matthew 11:28–30). All of them were *responsible* to come to him. Trask, so far as I know, refused to humble himself and believe the gospel. He rejected the message and chose the way of death. But Bob and Pauline believed with joy and entered into life.

What was the ultimate reason they chose Christ? Was it because they were wiser than Dr. Trask? Not at all. The difference was that God the Father had chosen to reveal these things not "to the wise and the prudent" but to "babies" (Matthew 11:25). Why God chose Bob, Pauline, and Jack we do not know; we can only wonder at such grace, such undeserved love.

Salvation always comes down to this, to what the theologians call God's sovereign grace. The phrase refers both to God's power and rule over all things, and the love and mercy in which he exercises that power. God plans our lives and orchestrates the details in such a way that we hear the gospel from people at just the right time. It is all part of a glorious program in which God is saving a number of people so vast that no one can count them.

When we talk to people about Jesus Christ, we don't need to figure out in advance which ones God is speaking to. Nor should we try to choose for God the ones he *should* reveal himself to! Our part is simply to share our faith with others, no matter how skeptical they might seem. Who knows whether we are talking to a Jack (the confirmed atheist), a Dr. Trask (the religious skeptic), or a Bob (the confused seeker)? Only God. It is our privilege simply to be partners with him as he opens the hearts of those who cross our paths.

Faith Looks for Prepared Hearts

CHAPTER SIX

Northern California, 1960

"You folks have a fine ranch here."

"We like it," Doris said.

"Wonder when Jack and your husband are coming back?"

"Never can tell," answered Doris.

Doris and I were leaning on a fence, admiring her ranch in the foothills of the Sierra Nevadas. Jack Julien, a friend from college, had a dental practice in nearby Sonora. He'd suggested that we drop in on his friends, Doris and Harry. No sooner had we arrived than Jack and Harry disappeared on a couple of Harry's horses. Jack loved horses. There was no telling when they'd be back.

Doris and I were standing and chatting by the corral, and I had run out of talk. How many times can you say to a woman dressed in jeans and boots, "You folks have a fine ranch here?"

I could have walked away and waited for Jack

73

by myself. But I was learning to expect that even chance meetings might reveal prepared hearts. Was there a way I could engage this woman with the gospel? I had grown up in a ranching family. Maybe we had some things in common. Were there questions that would open up her heart? I leaned on the Lord and plunged in.

Soon we were talking about horses. Doris, like my mother, was a born horsewoman. Mention something about horses and my mother came alive. The same thing happened with Doris. Soon I knew how many horses were on the ranch, the costs of feed, and the work of training them.

After about an hour I remarked that she was "a first rate observer of animals." Was this the way that God had prepared her heart? It was worth a try.

"What animals do you admire most?" I expected her to answer, "Horses."

But she said, "Pigs."

"Pigs?" I was surprised.

"Yes," she said with a half-smile. Then she launched into a long account of the behavior of pigs, describing their cleverness in getting their own way.

I responded, "It sounds like pigs act as if they had laws of behavior built inside them, and yet they can be inventive too."

She nodded, and then I asked, "Well, did you ever wonder how pigs got this way?"

She replied, "I don't know. Since I started watching them, I have been fascinated by them, but I never wondered how they got that way."

"Do you think that somebody made them?"

She said slowly and thoughtfully that she supposed it was impossible that pigs created themselves. They were too amazing and wonderful to have sprung out of the mud.

I told her what the Bible said about God's creation of animals. Then I asked her, "Did you ever notice how pigs behave better than many people?"

She laughed for the first time, open and freely. We had finally connected. It was obvious that in her mind, people did not stack up well against pigs. Now our interaction had reached the point where I could share the gospel. Her love for her animals had prepared the way.

"Well," I said, "people are worse than pigs. The Bible says that we are all born with a kink inside of us. It says that God created people good, but Adam and Eve sinned, and we all inherited a twisted mind because of what they did. That's why God sent Jesus, his Son, into the world to die for our kinkiness. In the Bible our bentness is called 'sin.'"

We were still talking about Jesus when Jack and Harry rode up. As we got in the car and drove away, Jack apologized, "I'm so sorry. I didn't mean to leave you talking with Doris for so long. I'm trying to decide whether to buy this horse, and just forgot about the time. What in the world did you talk about?"

"We talked about Jesus."

He almost stopped the car. He said, "Nobody talks to Doris about Jesus. When Christians come up here to share their faith, she drives them all away."

Turn up at Doris and Harry's ranch with a Bible in your hand, and Doris would show you the gate. Obviously, she had done so already to "visiting Christians" who had come to persuade her to "come to church." Remembering how I once felt about such an approach helped me avoid the mistake of beginning "too high up" with her.

Many people have had a bad experience in the past with "church." Perhaps they were bored when they were young, or felt that church was irrelevant to their lives as adults. Simply inviting them to church will most likely get you a no. I know how I once felt about people who carried Bibles. They made me nervous.

But over a number of years God had prepared my heart to hear the gospel, just as he had prepared Doris for our talk. The well-meaning Christians who would come to her door started "too high up" for her. Learning about God is a process. Love takes the trouble to listen and find out where a person is in that process.

Don't forget that God is in complete charge of it all. It was only in the previous couple of years that Doris had become fascinated by pigs. Three years before she might not have been ready even for my indirect approach. But then quietly God stirred her mind to see something new. Her growing capacity to see and wonder prepared her for our conversation. It was just our Father's timing, bringing to her a former atheist with a background similar to hers. As I saw and wondered with her, the barriers to biblical truth began to fall away.

I wasn't surprised when I encountered a prepared heart. I also thought church was boring when I was young, but over the years God had prepared my heart to hear the truth about myself and him.

No one could have started further from God than I did. When I was young, my father's death convinced me that the world was empty and without God. When an admired schoolteacher announced his atheism, my rebellious and angry heart responded. I became a committed atheist at twelve years old.

But over the years the Lord had challenged my atheism. He used different experiences to change my hard heart into a prepared heart. One fall day when I was fourteen, I was walking through the woods near my home. I stopped to admire a scene where a small creek edged its way out of the ancient rain forest and past a meadow. I had often paused just here. But this time, as the tall Douglas firs, the golden maples, and the moss-covered rocks captured my attention, I saw something that had escaped me until that moment.

It looked as if this scene had been *designed* to make a beautiful picture. Everything fit together in a way I'd never noticed before. I went away wondering, *Could this perfect design be the result of chance?* I wasn't sure.

I had more questions a year later when I was hunting north of town. I met a magnificent buck on a craggy ridge above the Rogue River. We were face to face and less than one hundred feet apart. I raised my rifle to shoot him. As he bounded away I had a perfect bead on him. But I did not shoot. I was so awed by his majesty that I could not pull the trigger.

At the time I did not think God had anything to do with my decision not to kill the buck. I only knew that I couldn't kill such a glorious animal. But if the buck had just evolved by chance, why would I care?

When I was sixteen, I dropped out of high school and left my home in Oregon. I moved to San Francisco to live with my sister Ella, who had become a Christian. There I was able to work in the shipyards and earn a high school diploma. My earlier questions prepared my heart to hear my sister Ella talk about God. Ella and I had many conversations about the meaning of life and her new faith.

During this same time, I saw a movie that

disturbed me. Its simple theme was that the problems of modern man stem from his inability to be thankful to God for his gifts of creation. This was a new thought for a confirmed atheist and another way God prepared my heart. The movie left me troubled and hungry for answers, and I began to attend church sporadically with my sister. Just as Doris's interest in pigs opened her to discussing God with me, so these events drew me towards God. Somewhat hesitantly I tried to read the Bible, but at first I was greatly repelled by it.

Then several weeks before World War II ended, we got word that my oldest brother Leo had been killed in Italy. Leo had thought that he might not return. Before he left he gave away all his personal possessions, including his prized gun. But to me, his death came as a tremendous shock. We had been very close. When my father died, Leo had taken me under his wing. After his death I was very alone. This is when I decided that my life wasn't working. I dropped out of college and returned to Oregon.

Even though I couldn't see it, God was using these things to prepare me for the summer when I finally put my trust in Christ. Only by such a series of hard, slow steps did I make the journey from atheism to a life of faith. As I began to live this new life, I found out that God was going to continue preparing my heart, both to learn more about him and also to share him with others.

This life of faith opened up a whole new world to me. I now had a beautiful wife who shared my love for God. Together we began to raise a family. I wanted to be partners with Rose Marie not only in raising a family, but also in ministry. So after college I attended seminary. I thought that I knew quite a bit about the Christian faith and how to share it. But the Lord had many more things to teach me. Sometimes I encountered prepared hearts and didn't know what to do with them.

By 1960 I was teaching high school English at a Christian school in central California. At the same time I was recruited by my pastor to plant a church in Stockton, California. I was also working on my doctorate at a nearby university. Rose Marie and I had five children. Life was hectic!

By this time I had a great deal of training and Christian experience, but much of my joy was gone. I realized there was something wrong with me when I was planting that church in California. Without realizing it, I had stopped knowing how to respond to a prepared heart.

One day I was driving down the street, and I heard some noise from the parking lot of a fast-food place. A white-haired old lady pulling a market basket behind her was walking down the street. Eight or ten boys were throwing stones at her and yelling. I couldn't believe my ears! Being a good Boy Scout from Oregon, where we helped old ladies across the street, I was enraged! I had forgotten that for years I had been an atheist and a wild kid myself.

I turned into the drive-in and then had a moment of fear. I wondered if maybe I should get a hamburger and a milkshake and rethink this. I had never done anything like this before. But my indignation was stronger than my fear. I went over to the boys—God gave me grace—I didn't pray, I just went over there. Perhaps I went in my own strength, but God did help me.

I asked them if they had ever heard of the fifth commandment. It was news to them—they had never heard of "Honor your father and mother" (Deuteronomy 5:16). When I applied it to older people and authorities, they were even more amazed. I started preaching to them and then was in a predicament. I couldn't figure out how to end. I was afraid of what they might do when I stopped! Finally, in desperation, I pointed to our church steeple down the street and said, "I expect to see all of you in church on Sunday." (I didn't, really.)

But the leader and one of his friends did come to church on Sunday morning. They sat down in the back while we all tried not to stare. Their leather jackets and boots were in sharp contrast to our suits, high heels, and hats. But even though they hadn't known the fifth commandment, their arrival meant that God was at work. God can prepare even the hardest heart to hear his truth. Unfortunately, I really didn't know what to do with these prepared hearts. And I knew that my church didn't know what to do with them either.

At this time in my life, I was preoccupied with ministry, finances, family, and all the rest. There was no overflow of joy. The boys' hearts may have been prepared, but mine was not. I didn't know what to say to them and I never saw them again.

What had happened to me? Without my noticing, my own heart had hardened. I felt disconnected from grace; I hadn't been like that as a young Christian. Have you ever had an experience where God richly blessed you and then, instead of going on with it, you stagnated? That is where I was. I had lost the sense that I was in partnership with the Father, and I had lost the sense that God could change any heart.

I was right to stop my car and challenge those young men with the law of God. God blessed what I did, but all I gave them was the law. All I expressed was my own indignation at *their* breaking of the law, without any sense of indignation over the way I did the same. I didn't say, "Fellas, I'm a lot like you. I used to be *just* like you. I didn't tease old ladies, but I probably did things that were worse in God's eyes."

I couldn't say this to these young men because, without knowing it, I had come to think that I was a pretty good person. In my pride I thought I was better than they were. I had forgotten what Paul said in Romans, "There is no difference, all have sinned and come short of the glory of God" (Romans 3:22–23). I had broken the law of God by failing to love these boys.

Not until years later, after the Lord had restored my relationship to himself, did I know how to respond to this kind of prepared heart. But God is in the business of preparing hearts. He had prepared my heart to receive grace and now he was going to prepare me to be the type of pastor who could offer grace to others. Somehow in the years since Tony, Mel, and John, I had lost my sense that God's power and love were for everyone. Why could I engage Doris, but not the young men at the drive-in?

God's sovereignty in salvation means that God is irresistibly drawing his sheep to himself as part of a process, sometimes a long one. I could see that Doris was somewhere in that process, but I had written off the young men at the drive-in. I was wrong in that.

As part of that process God reveals himself through human experiences as the God who made us and seeks us. I knew that from my own experience. Doris' interest in the created world was God's way of revealing himself to her. God also wanted to reveal himself to those young men through my testimony. Unfortunately, I was too self-righteous and too unbelieving to give it to them.

There is no automatic way to know where people are in their life story, so we need to ask God to show us. Then we have to believe by faith that he will give us the wisdom and the grace that we need to speak.

What I couldn't see in Stockton was that God was looking into my life. He could see where I was. He could see the kind of things I needed to experience in order to renew my desire to bring Christ to all kinds of people.

By his grace he would give those things to me.

Living Water for the Thirsty

CHAPTER SEVEN

Bucks County, Pennsylvania, 1964–1970

The year 1964 introduced a decade of change for me and my family. That year we left California and moved to Pennsylvania, so that I could teach at a seminary near Philadelphia. My family did not want to move, but I thought I would be better at teaching seminary than at sharing the gospel with rock-throwing young toughs. But even though I liked teaching seminary, I missed the pastorate. So when a small country church offered me a part-time position, I accepted. Soon we were commuting twenty miles every Sunday to a small chapel in Bucks County.

These commitments meant that I was spending most of my time with church members and seminary students. Naturally I assumed that they had already experienced a changed life. But I was to find out that many of them did not have a personal relationship with the God of the universe.

It was, then, a time of surprises. Some of the

surprises were unpleasant and stemmed from my pastoral failures. Donna, one of the young adults at the chapel, was one of those failures. She left us to join another church group. I was sorry to see her go and asked her why she had left.

She was glad to tell me. "I became a Christian at this other fellowship. They asked me hard questions about the real me. I didn't like it at first. Here no one—including you—asked what I was really like. You were kind to me, but you didn't ask the tougher questions. I had been calling myself a Christian and giving all the Christian answers when secretly I was doing a lot of wrong stuff and wasn't a Christian at all."

Her explanation was pretty devastating. She was telling me that I was nice, but naive about soul care. I had failed her, and felt the shame of it. Aware that I was listening to her, she added that she thought I was too quick to accept people at face value.

Was I? It was a troubling question. I had others as well. Why couldn't I see below the surface in her life? Why did I expect so little change from the young people in my congregation?

Some of my pastoral successes were as puzzling as my failures. As I rode in the car one day with a pillar of the church, we had a strange conversation. Bud, a successful businessman and church leader, wanted to talk about a sermon I had preached on "Blessed Are the Poor in Spirit." It had shaken his way of thinking about himself and Christianity. He concluded, "I came to this church convinced I was a live Christian, an evangelical who knew the gospel and had received Christ. But I now see that my pride was never touched by Christ. Inside I was still full of envy and greed. You know, for a conversion to be real, there must be a breaking down of pride, and this is happening to me. Christ is real to me for the first time."

I couldn't deny that Bud had changed. And neither could the rest of the people in his world. A business colleague commented on his transformation by saying, "I don't know how or why, but whatever you did to him, keep it up!"

What was happening? One church member left to become a believer at another church while another church member had just now become a believer. *What was I missing?*

What I was missing, I know now, was the expectation that lives of faith will be changed lives. I had expected too little from Donna and from Bud. I was content with surface reformations.

But now I wanted more from God than superficial change. As I pored over the word of God, it seemed to promise so much more than what I saw happening in my own life and in the Christian community. Once again I was in that desperate position that had first caused me to trust in Christ.

The first symptom of that desperation was a deep discouragement that I experienced in the winter and spring of 1970. I was frustrated and angry with myself for not being able to bring change to others. I was mad at those "others" for not changing despite my best efforts. In my pride, I resigned from my teaching position and from my pastorate. I cried for two weeks—in self-pity.

But the Spirit convicted me of my own arrogance and lack of faith. I saw that I was consumed by the desire to have a successful ministry, but I couldn't get my parishioners and students to cooperate. Finally I realized that I was expecting them to have a life of repentance and faith that I didn't have myself.

I saw depths of pride in myself that shocked me. I discovered that my pride expressed itself in people-pleasing and an avoidance of rejection. The plain truth is that I was a proud church leader who did not want to get hurt by his fellow Christians. I was expecting others to change in ways that I had not.

I had to face up to what I had done. I had resigned out of frustration and anger. I realized that I had not loved the people I was working with—I had only judged them. Now I needed to apologize. So I visited each of my colleagues on the seminary staff and admitted my pride and expressed my repentance. Faculty and friends in the church urged me to take back my resignations, so I did.

But I needed more than repentance. I also needed faith—specifically, faith in the promises that I had been reading about when all this turmoil began. Leaving the area for the summer of 1970, I used the time to study the promises of the Bible with new intensity. I traced them through Scripture with care, and even made a chart of what I found. I was astonished by the abundance of grace promised to sinners from Genesis to Revelation. My inward self longed with increasing passion to taste the life and power promised in the Bible and to see that kind of life formed in others.

I saw these promises as God's commitment to making big, deep-down changes in people's lives. Wanting this for my ministry, I memorized John 7:37–39:

> On the last and greatest day of the Feast, Jesus stood and said in a loud voice, "If anyone is thirsty, let him come to me and drink. Whoever believes in me, as the Scripture has said, streams of living water will flow from within him." By this he meant the Spirit, whom those who believed in him were later to receive. Up to that time the Spirit had not been given, since Jesus had not yet been glorified. (NIV)

As I read Jesus' promise to give overflowing water to the thirsty, I knew that I was certainly thirsty and that others were too.

The first thing that changed was my prayer life. When I felt discouraged and depressed, I had used this as an excuse not to pray. But discouragement and depression were not the real hindrances to my prayers. What hindered my prayer life was pride and unbelief. I thought I could do it all (pride), and I didn't really think that anybody was going to change (unbelief).

The discouragement and depression were fruits of those deeper sins.

Now, it is natural to feel our weakness when we try to pray, but sometimes we see this weakness as a reason *not* to pray. This is a mistake. True, when I look at my praying, my mind fills up with awareness of weakness. But my incapacity becomes an advantage when I relate my need to God's promises. My emptiness is what the Lord promises to fill with living water. It took the near collapse of my career to show me my emptiness.

That summer a change took place. Now when I prayed I expected God to change me and other people. This is what the promises of God were all about. Instead of seeing the people I was teaching and ministering to as enemies, I began to see that they were as thirsty for living water as I was. I saw that as we drank of God's promises together, we would begin to change. What I didn't know was how contagious it would be when "good" people began to repent of their superficial goodness and their underlying pride, greed, and arrogance.

I got an inkling of this when I was asked (pushed?) into going with a group of seminary students to street preach in New York City. I didn't want to go. I was prejudiced against street preaching: it evoked images of a single man standing on a corner, speaking into the wind with no one listening.

But these students knew how depressed I had been and insisted that I come. They knew what I didn't. With most of my time spent at seminary and church, I needed the challenge of talking about my faith in a new setting. And they assured me that they had a different approach to street preaching. "We go to places where there are crowds of people, and we take a group of fifteen to twenty Christians to form a core listening group."

I wondered on the drive to New York who was going to preach. But guess what? When I arrived at "our" spot near Greenwich Village, I discovered that I was going to be the preacher, and no excuses would be accepted. The students were unanimous. Believe me, I was suddenly thirsting for grace. I heard Jesus' words deep in my empty heart, "If anyone is thirsty, let him come to me and drink. Whoever believes, . . . streams of living water will flow from within him. By this he meant the Spirit [who] . . . had not [yet] been given . . ." (John 7:37–39 NIV).

When I climbed up on the small stand, I spoke as loudly as I could about "living water for the thirsty." To my amazement, people gathered to hear me. As I watched them cross over from a parkway to listen, I felt deep joy because I knew the Spirit was drawing them.

At one point, to the amusement of my students, I said, "Oh, the bliss of knowing Jesus Christ personally!" This archaic religious language reflected my joy and probably some lingering nervousness. In spite of its complete inappropriateness for my audience, this word "bliss" described what the Spirit was bringing into my life. I meant it from the heart. The depression and self-pity were gone. I was inexpressibly happy.

While my hearers looked momentarily puzzled, they kept on listening, and soon some of the students and I were down on our knees, praying with a man who had been heckling me earlier. Behind his surface hostility lived a thirsty human being who had been prepared by the Spirit. He said that he wanted to receive Christ and afterwards agreed to be discipled by local Christians.

This street preaching was not an isolated incident. In the years to come I would preach this way in Philadelphia, Kampala, Amsterdam, London, and Moscow and see many people's lives change.

I didn't know that at the time. But I could see that whereas all had been frustration and dryness, now there were change and new beginnings.

Some of those changes occurred at seminary. In the fall of 1970, I taught a Tuesday evening course. One night after class, one of my students, Roger, approached me to ask about a very sick young woman who had recently been converted at the chapel. I told him the same thing I had mentioned in class. "She is very sick, but the joy is strong. Even when she cannot speak, her face has joy written on it."

Roger and I sat in my car, both of us moved as we reflected on what God was doing in the life of this new Christian. Roger then asked me a question. "Can you be a Christian without the fruit of the Spirit?"

I asked him to explain what he meant. He said, "In your lectures you keep talking about streams of living water flowing through the believer, and it seems that this has to do with the fruit of the Spirit. Well, if that's right, I'm wondering about myself. I don't really see evidence of 'love, joy, and peace' in my life. What do you think? Is it possible that I may not be a Christian?"

I said cautiously, "Well, if a person really does not have any of the fruit of the Spirit in his life, that person would not be a Christian."

We talked more about the nature of the "fruit of the Spirit." Roger finally concluded, "I don't see 'streams of living water' coming from me."

The next morning Roger found me and continued his questioning while we waited in line for coffee. He remarked that if he compared himself to Moses and Jonah in the Bible, he knew he resembled Jonah. He said, "Moses was willing to die for the people, but Jonah ran away. I just don't love people. Even my witnessing has not been witnessing, but beating people over the head with the Bible."

We sat down in the lounge with our coffee, and suddenly Roger said, "I feel like someone is picking at a thick crust. I am the thick crust, and it's God who's doing the picking. I'm going to . . . pray." Now our seminary is not an austere place, but like most schools, the faculty and students often have a conventional reserve. I know I have mine. I was completely unprepared for what happened next.

Roger fell to his knees and, in the presence of all of us coffee drinkers, he began to pray. Tears were running down his face.

After a time he stood up and said, "I think I just got converted." The tears were still flowing. Streams of living water?

I was speechless. In my whole life I never had a conversation even remotely resembling this one.

But I was going to have more conversations like this. Roger came to our church, told his story, and immediately a young high school teacher named Michael ran across the auditorium to talk with him about these "streams of living water." Michael and I talked together too, and soon I could see that his life had changed like Roger's.

Next, Roger gathered a good-sized group of his seminary friends on campus and told them his story. He raised a question for them. "Is it possible that some of you may not really have been converted?" Roger now had the courage to ask those hard questions that I hadn't even thought to ask Donna and Bud. In response, a number of other seminarians came to talk to me about their relationship with Christ.

Stan was a student who came to speak with me after another Tuesday evening class. I had spoken on James 4:1–10, the theme, "Grace Runs Downhill to the Humble." My mind had been captured by the promise stated in James 4:6: "God opposes the proud but gives grace to the humble" (NIV). There is a strong warning in this passage directed to the proud, but it seemed to me that in light of the context, this verse is a promise of abundant grace to those who humble themselves.

I had taken hold of this promise, and now in my weakness I was inviting others to do the same. I was saying that the normal Christian life was one filled with grace, obtained by weak people as they relied on the promises of God.

Stan told me that he was convinced that he had never known Christ. "I am," he said with grief, "full of pride." After a time of painful soul-searching, Stan confessed that in the past he had persecuted born-again believers in his church. He thought they were strange and contemptible, but now he was conscience-stricken.

With my encouragement he studied Isaiah 53 and rested his life on Christ, who was "pierced for our transgressions" (v. 5 NIV). Stan then became another weak person receiving grace through the promises, and his joy in the message of the cross stimulated others to seek grace too.

At the same time, God was also working powerfully at the chapel. Over the next eight months, my Monday evening Bible study grew from a dozen people to more than sixty and was still growing. Many new people, including some non-Christians, came to the Wednesday evening prayer meeting. Eventually more people were coming than had come to the Sunday morning service when I first became pastor. What I had failed to do on my own, God was doing as he had promised.

One Wednesday evening in the summer of 1971, the prayer meeting overflowed with people, so small groups went out onto the church lawn to pray. Attracted by the sounds and sights of life, a carload of high school students stopped to investigate. Within a couple of months, one of them—the president of the student council in his high school—gave his life to Christ and became active in our church.

I was now asking the right questions. God in his mercy had given me a caring boldness. I was now willing to accept the loss of popularity in order to help people come to know Christ.

Not everyone was pleased with the working of grace in people's lives. A young man in his early twenties became a believer through the Bible study. His mother had begun to attend the chapel with him, and I had asked her whether she felt a work of grace was going on in her life. She was offended and became so hostile that, according to her later testimony, she gave negative reports about me for the next two years. But at the end of that time, she was still haunted by the questions I had asked her and suddenly could bear the pressure no longer. She was passing a church building where a Billy Graham film was being shown, went in, and received Christ.

She wrote me a beautiful letter thanking me for having the courage to ask her about grace in her life and loving her enough to endure the pain she caused me. She was right—it had been painful.

It was the kind of pain that I had avoided at all costs when I had started this pastorate. However, it was part of my Father's sovereign plan. He wanted to kill in me the love of human praise. By now I was getting more and more acclamation, so this persecution kept me honest. To endure it, I constantly had to humble myself and seek grace. It was this humbling that kept my ministry alive.

D. T. Niles has said that "evangelism is one poor beggar telling another poor beggar where to find bread." This is a wonderful definition. But now I wanted to add something to this insight. Evangelism is also one hungry beggar eagerly *eating* the bread and being changed by it, and then telling the other poor beggars to eat of the same bread.

Learning that I was a poor beggar who needed to lean daily on the promises of God changed my whole life and ministry. I stood by in awe as I watched streams of living water flow into the lives of the people around me. I also watched as my church came to life. Streams of living water were flowing from them to the people around them. Soon the chapel was bursting at the seams with people. Our Bible studies and prayer meetings attracted unchurched young people—some of them like the student council president and others who struggled with drug addiction and favored alternative lifestyles.

Roger was correct. You cannot be a Christian without any fruit of the Spirit. But by humbling yourself and leaning on the promises of grace, you can be sure you will have the Spirit working these fruits in you. As the Spirit breaks down your self-dependence and pride, you will become part of a chain of grace. Other weak people will see your thirsting and drinking of Christ through faith in his gospel, and they will want to drink too.

It is important to see that the Bible promises the presence of the Spirit throughout its pages. One of the important images used in Scripture to stimulate our faith and witness is the promise of the abundant "pouring" of the Spirit on the needy, the helpless, and the sinful. Here are some of the passages that built my own faith: Exodus 17:1–7; Isaiah 32:15–20; 44:1–5; 54:1–11; Ezekiel 47:1–12; Joel 2:28–32; Zechariah 12:10–13:1; 14:8; John 1:29, 33; 4:10, 14; 7:37–39; 19:34; 1 John 5:6–8; Revelation 22:17.

At the end of this decade of turmoil, something new emerged. No longer was the church I pastored only for "churchgoers." Now we could see a true picture of the kingdom of God there. Business suits sat next to leather jackets on Sunday morning. The churchgoers themselves had experienced a deep-down change. The hallmark of their lives was no longer pride and self-righteousness. Instead it was humility, love, and joy. They opened their homes and their hearts to the young people in their community, and streams of living water flowed. The streams of living water were attracting all kinds of people from all walks of life, just as God had promised.

A Faith for Fathers, Sons, and Orphans

CHAPTER EIGHT

Jenkintown, Pennsylvania, 1972

Over a period of several years, God had used my depression over ministry failures to break me of my pride and self-sufficiency. The Spirit of God had renewed my confidence in his promise to change people, and more and more I was learning to ground my ministry in expectant prayer. By 1972, I had resigned as pastor of the Chapel (this time for more positive reasons than I'd had a few years before), but I still wanted a way to share my new joy with people. I especially wanted to reach my own community in the Philadelphia suburbs. With that in mind, Rose Marie and I started a prayer meeting in our living room. It grew rapidly. When we outgrew the living room, we moved to the local library and started a worship service there.

How nice it would have been if God had had no more to teach me! But God's plans always involve deepening the life of faith in his children. I had learned to share my faith with all kinds of people—but had I shared it with my own family?

I had cause to wonder. The previous year our daughter Barbara had moved out of the circle of our family and church, and then announced that she was "not a Christian anymore." I was stunned; I felt numb. At first I rejected her assessment, but eventually, I had no choice but to take her at her word.

Though I was now a "successful" pastor and church planter, I didn't have a clue as to how to reach *this* non-Christian who was so dear to me. I was the one who was supposed to know how to share the gospel with *anybody,* but every time I tried to talk to Barbara, it ended in frustration for both of us. I had lost a daughter and a close friend. It hurt.

Around that time, I asked my wife, Rose Marie, "If there was one thing about me that you could change, what would it be?"

She answered right away, "Jack, you don't listen." Her reply astonished me. Didn't I always pay close attention and then offer her my excellent advice? Finally, I saw what she meant. She wanted loving, patient listening. She wanted me to give up my instinctive tendency to interrupt and correct from the standpoint of my imagined superiority. Her criticism hurt, but it was good pain, healing surgery done by the Spirit of Christ. I needed to hear what she had to say— but I still didn't know how to change.

It just wasn't easy actually to change my tendency to correct and control Rose Marie. So I went to the Bible, where I had always gone when I was troubled. I needed to clear my head of confusion and guilt and once again I felt the deep need to hear the voice of my Father.

I began by making a careful study of the law of God in the Old Testament. Just what did the Lord expect of me as a husband? I concluded that the law demanded from me a perfect love for my wife (my neighbor). Before Rose Marie had spoken to me, I had assumed that I had that kind of love for her. But I didn't. Too often I acted as her judge, not her lover, and the Bible says this is a rotten thing to do (James 4:11–12).

God's law says flat out, "Love your neighbor as yourself" (Leviticus 19:18 NIV). For me that meant *Love your wife with a total commitment and stop trying to dominate her.* The law's exposure of my judgmental perfectionism left me depressed. It had crushed some cherished illusions about my own goodness.

I had now been a Christian for more than twenty years, but these truths about God's requirements showed me that I needed to go deeper in my relationships with those closest to me.

In my search for God's wisdom, I turned to the book of Galatians. There I read that Christ had fully borne the law's condemnation of me, and I was now connected to this truth by faith. I could have jumped for joy! I saw the seriousness of my sin but I no longer felt the terrible guilty burden of having failed my wife.

In fact, I now heard the gospel message as God's great *YES* over my whole life—past, present, and future. God was pleased with me because Jesus' death had taken away the condemnation I deserved, and it had also taken away God's anger toward me. I was his son forever. I was no longer a slave or an orphan. It was time to stop acting like an orphan and to start loving my family the way God loved me.

I needed to apply what I had learned to my family relationships. If God accepts me as his son, then I can accept others in the same way, especially Rose Marie and the rest of my family. I can forget about myself, humble myself, and find my joy in serving them from the heart.

What did this mean practically in my family? For starters, I had to imitate my Father: he is not my condemner; instead he is now my affirmer. He is *for* me forever, without any hidden reservations because I am now connected to Christ, his Son, by faith. I am in Christ, and his righteousness is mine.

Thus my calling is to imitate my Father. I must no longer condemn my wife, and I must be willing to apologize when I become critical of her. What's more, I must affirm and praise her like mad!

This was not natural to me. Like many other Christian leaders, I have gotten my share of criticism, but I have also received a great deal of praise and affirmation. It is embarrassing to admit, but it is easy to drift into taking the acclamation seriously, seeing oneself as a noble leader reaching down from moral heights to help less fortunate beings.

But my family saw me as I really was, and if God's work was to continue in my life, I needed to start listening to them. My fresh awareness of God's unconditional love finally gave me the strength to do so.

The Holy Spirit was now stirring me to listen to my wife and to praise and affirm her. It was only a small beginning, but it *was* a beginning. I wondered, after years of my acting as her critic and judge, would she doubt my sincerity? The answer was no. She loved it!

During this time, I had a speaking engagement at a church in the South. During Sunday school I was explaining how to share the Christian faith with friends and neighbors using a booklet I had written, "Have you ever wanted A NEW LIFE?" I started by stressing that sin is primarily human self-centeredness and a resulting thanklessness (see Appendix A, page 143). I explained that a thankless, self-centered life makes it impossible to love Jesus and the people close to you. I concluded that people who are not thankful to God for his gifts cannot love one another—and they certainly can't love Jesus. Just ask them a question: "Did you ever stop doing a

single thing because you love Jesus? Or start doing a single thing just because you love him?"

At that moment one of the men in the class
stood up and hurried to the back of the church.
I thought he was sick, so I pursued him after
class to see if he was all right. He was not all
right. He said that my words about thankfulness
to God and love to Jesus tore him apart. "I don't
have any of it," he said, and with that he disappeared out the door of the church. I had to wait
until after I had preached my sermon to talk to
him again.

After the service, there was a telephone call
asking the pastor and me to come to his home.
When we arrived at the home of this family counselor, we found the door open and went in. We
found him hugging his wife and crying.

"Don't worry," his wife said. "It's all good. He
went to church this morning and came home a
changed man. I don't know what you did to him,
but for the first time in our marriage, I have a
loving, tender husband."

The man stopped weeping, smiled, and told
us a remarkable story. He had assumed that he
was a Christian. He was a faithful church member, he thought he understood the gospel, and he
joined the evangelism class to learn how to share
the good news. Then that morning he saw for the
first time that the cross was not especially good
news to him. He was not grateful to God for all of
his gifts, and he was especially ungrateful for the

gift of his wife. He was her judge, not her loving husband; her accuser, not her friend.

For the first time he saw what sin really was, and what Christ had done on the cross for a real live sinner who did not love either his wife or Jesus. God broke him. Now he did not seem to be able to stop hugging his wife.

This man was now deeply thankful for the message of the cross. He had seen his sin of thanklessness to the God who had given him his wife. Before, he would have said that Christ died for sinners; now he could say, "Christ died for me."

It was amazing for me to see the gospel change both my marriage and the marriages of people like this family counselor. It gave me new hope as I looked at my other family relationships. In particular I was concerned for Barbara, who was still living in a "far country." Because of that I went to her and asked, with fear and trembling, "Barb, what do you have against me?"

She was surprised but soon she replied, "Dad, you're too perfect, and nobody is that perfect." I apologized and asked her to forgive me for my pride and self-righteousness. She did, and we wept together. Though our relationship had a long way to go, it was now on the mend. My family was beginning to see that the gospel could even change their father!

I wasn't the only father changed by this gospel of grace. Not long after my talk with Barbara, a father and a son came to me for counseling. We were seated together in our living room, when the son looked at his father and said, with great bitterness, "Dad is a hypocrite. He pretends he's religious, but he really does not practice it except on Sunday. He does not know how to love people. He feels superior to me and looks down on me. He does not really believe anything, he is just putting on a show."

This young man's indictment of his father, a distinguished professional man, was devastating. I had been raised with a respect for authority. In my generation, sons didn't talk like that! I asked the son, "How can you say these things about your father? They can't be true." I was so troubled that I wanted to stop the meeting.

But then the upset father said, "He's right. It's all true, and worse. Let him continue."

His son was not using swear words, but he was virtually cursing his dad, and it went on a long time. Finally the father broke under this tongue lashing, and in tears he asked his son to forgive him. Then I said to both of them, father and son, "Galatians 3:13 says that Jesus took away the curse of the law by becoming a curse for us on the cross."

I didn't know if this teaching would mean anything to either one of them. Since neither of them said much, I went on to explain that the son had acted very much like the law of God. He had condemned his dad for his sins, and the law does the same for all of us. From the perspective of the law we are *all* hypocrites who do not know how to love people. Instead we put on a show to cover up our contempt for others.

I continued, "We are all under the curse of the law. We all have betrayed others and God. We have not loved our neighbor or our God. But," I added, "there's no more anger against us if we connect ourselves to Christ by faith. Faith is saying yes to Christ, like getting married. We receive him, and his death and perfect righteousness cover all our sins. From this moment on we are no longer cursed by the law and we no longer curse each other."

The son said little; he just watched his father. With deep brokenness the father then prayed to receive Christ. Before the long evening was over, the father was filled with joy and warmly hugged a son who hardly knew what to do with his new dad. But I did. I hugged the dad. We two sinners wept together, laughed, and hugged each other some more. Who would have expected that the son's bitter cursing would be used by God to expose the father—and me—to our unloving, curse-deserving hearts?

It was strange to watch God answering our prayers. Here an angry son acted like the voice of the law, thundering wrath at his parent. I do not excuse the son's bitterness, but the Spirit of God used him to expose his father's tendency to trivialize his sin and to convict him that his sin is a betrayal of God. I felt exposed as well. My prayers and those of many others had been answered with God's power. He was "convicting the world of sin" through his Spirit (John 16:8–9).

As I saw the power of God to change me, my family, and others, I wanted more than anything to share this with the rest of the world. In the disconnected young people I saw all around me, I saw orphans who needed a father desperately. I wanted to meet them any way I could.

Some of them were finding their way to our young church, which we called New Life Presbyterian. We purposely met at 4:30 in the afternoon to accommodate their lifestyle. Dress was casual, music was contemporary, open sharing was the order of the day. I was the only one who wore a tie.

But holding services wasn't enough: I wanted to seek these orphans out. Rose Marie and I got into the habit of stopping for hitchhikers whenever we could, and then sharing our faith with our captive audience.

One day we were late getting started for a drive to Washington, D.C. As I crossed the railway bridge near our home, I was determined to make up for lost time. But as I stopped at the traffic light, I saw a teenager standing on the corner thumbing a ride. My first thought was, *I just don't have time to give him a lift.* My second thought was, *God has been so good to me, I have to stop.* Moments later the teenager was sitting in the back seat of our green Nova.

We found that we had a cool guy on our hands, one who forcefully corrected our mistaken impression that he came from the local alternative high school. In response to his questions, I introduced myself. "I teach at a seminary. My wife and I have opened our home to all kinds of people. We often have people stay with us to work through hard problems."

He said, "You really have people live with you? Why?"

I answered, "We believe Jesus came into the world to bring people a new life, and we want them to see that he's for real." We briefly told him about some of the people who had lived with us. By this time we had reached our hitchhiker's destination, but he made no effort to leave. He sat there for another fifteen minutes, mostly just listening to us. He then left with a "New Life" booklet in his hand. To be honest, I never expected to see him again.

But as our church prayed together, I found that I wasn't alone in my desire to reach this generation with the love of Christ. Some of the seminary students who had experienced renewal now wanted to share their faith with all kinds of people. After our prayer meetings we would go out to bars, street corners, and drive-ins to talk to young people about Christ. Because we had a woman living with us who was involved in a motorcycle gang, I decided we should seek out some of those gang members.

What happened is a humbling lesson in how *not* to approach groups of possibly hostile people. I and my pastoral assistant, Ron Lutz, drove to a nearby drive-in one hot summer night about four months after meeting our hitchhiker. Contrary to what I had been told, there were no motorcycle gang members present, but about fifty older teenagers were there, most of them drunk or high.

I drove into the parking lot between two large groups. I stepped out of my car and said, "Hi, I'm Rev. Miller and I'm looking for a motorcycle gang." I had instant attention—none of it favorable. I was immediately surrounded by hostile young people who wanted to drive off "the holy Joe."

The conversation went from bad to worse. A tall wiry fellow named Davy was drunk and cursing. We argued a bit. Then I blundered unwittingly. I had purchased a large, chocolate-coated soft ice cream and while these young people were arguing and partly jeering at me, melting chocolate and soft ice cream started dripping over my fingers and down my arms, and I said, "This isn't getting me anywhere."

Davy thought I was talking about my conversation with him and he felt insulted. He just seemed to go crazy. With outstretched arms lifted to the sky, he screamed at the top of his lungs that he was ready to get a gun and start killing people "like the guy did from the tower in Texas."

His cursing and threats angered me, and for a moment I self-righteously wanted to get even. But I repented of my anger, and just stood there quietly, listening to him yell, praying for him, and expecting God to hear my prayers. What God did was to take condemnation out of my heart, and that freedom enabled me to endure his hostility.

Davy, in effect, was saying no to God. But I remembered that once I had too. So I just refused to leave and waited for God to work.

He did. Suddenly, out of the night, came the wildest teenager of them all. He had a quart beer bottle in one hand, and with the other he began hitting Davy and swinging him around in a weird dance through the crowds of teenagers.

Soon he stopped near me, and came over to investigate. I smiled and said, "I'm Dr. Miller." (It seemed to me that Rev. Miller had not gone over well, and so I opted for a little dignity.)

He said, grinning and swaying, "Not John Miller?"

I answered, "Well, maybe, yes."

"Don't you recognize me?" he asked with a laugh. "I'm Bob Heppe. You picked me up a few weeks ago and gave me a lift. I've been calling your house."

"Why?" I asked cautiously.

"I want to find out if you are for real."

We talked some more, and then he seemed satisfied, and yelled at the teenagers to gather around. They came willingly when he told them that I was his friend and could be trusted. Next he divided them into two groups, one group for me and one group for Ron. Then he said, "They're O.K. Listen to them. I'm going to." Ron and I pulled out "New Life" booklets and told them about Christ.

For several months I kept coming to the drive-in on Wednesday night after prayer meeting and on Saturday nights after I was finished working on my sermon. Bob was always there. Then, because of work at seminary and the church, I missed going to the drive-in for ten days. On my next trip Bob wasn't there, so I stopped by his house to see how he was. I found him lying on the couch in his living room, with an open Bible on the coffee table. His eyes were clear, and he looked different. I asked him, "Have you become a Christian?"

He replied, "I think so. I've been sober since I last saw you, and I can't remember when I've been sober that long." He was right. He had become a believer in Jesus Christ, and he was no longer a disconnected orphan. He had become a son of God and my brother.

Soon Rick Buddemeier, a seminary student, began to disciple Bob through the process of leaving behind his abuse of alcohol and drugs. Over the next two years Bob repaid business people and others from whom he had stolen and became an honors student at Temple University.

The amazing end to this story is that eventually Bob fell in love with my youngest daughter, Keren. Bob, the former drug addict, married my beautiful blonde daughter on a sunny afternoon in October 1981. The disconnected orphan had become not only the son of God, but also my son.

Together we have shared our faith in Africa, Ireland, England, and, of course, Philadelphia. He became an elder at our church, New Life Presbyterian, and now he, Keren, and their four children are missionaries in London. Could there be a better illustration of how the living water of the gospel makes orphans into sons?

God had brought me a long way since that day in California when I didn't know how to share his love with the kids who were tormenting the elderly woman at the drive-in. God had taught me through my struggles with my family, that I was just like them. I needed God's grace just as much as they did. As I lived and taught this truth to others, I now had a church family that not only warmly welcomed the orphans, but was willing to seek them out. It was our great privilege to see God bring the orphans and transform them into our brothers and sisters.

The glory of God is the difference between what we would naturally do and what grace accomplishes in our lives through the death of Christ. By his grace he rescues us from a natural state in which we are condemned by his law and yet constantly defend ourselves and condemn others. Christ comes and writes his great, ever-lasting *yes* over our new lives. Praise him for the difference!

The power to share our faith humbly and effectively then comes from our sure knowledge that we are God's sons and daughters. This knowledge takes root as we carefully and constantly apply the message of the cross to our own consciences. We learn that the message of the cross is God's *yes* over us, and as we confess our sins, we are enabled to bear open and confident witness out of our knowledge of our Father's daily cleansing. It is a glorious message, and it is our privilege to share it.

Faith Learns to Love Strangers

CHAPTER NINE

Philadelphia, 1996

The early years of New Life Church were the beginning of great things. God grew the prayer meeting that met in our living room into a network of churches in the Philadelphia area. Seminary students who worked with me at the start of New Life went on to pastor their own churches, both here and abroad. Ron Lutz, the pastoral assistant who bravely accompanied me to the drive-in, now pastors New Life Presbyterian Church in Fort Washington. There are many others like him.

God has also spread that little prayer meeting beyond the Philadelphia area. In the early 1970s, Ugandan refugees began coming to New Life church. When we heard about the spiritual and physical needs in their homeland, I began to take short-term mission teams to Kampala, the capital city of Uganda. Eventually this led to the founding of World Harvest Mission, which now has missionaries in Africa, Europe, India, and the former Soviet Union. As the mission has grown, my role as director requires me to spend more of my time overseas, encouraging our missionaries and writing. I also spend a good deal of time speaking on renewal issues to churches across the United States.

I am excited to see God working overseas and in churches here, although my schedule leaves me fewer free moments to share my faith. But when I travel, I always have a captive audience in the people who are unfortunate enough to sit next to me and Rose Marie. I learned some years back from a good friend that it is possible to interest complete strangers in the gospel message without being offensive.

Early in my ministry at New Life Church, my friend Will and I made plans to go to Philadelphia on a midmorning train. He was to board at Glenside, one stop before mine. When I climbed on the train in Jenkintown, I did not see him anywhere.

What I did see left me astonished. Everyone in my car had a small pamphlet and everyone seemed to be reading it. I went to the next car and saw the same thing: people reading what turned out to be Christian pamphlets.

Baffled, I sat down. By now I had figured out that Will must have handed out the reading material, but how did he get so many commuters to read it?

A few minutes later Will came into the car, saw me, grinned broadly, and sat down next to me. I said with a laugh, "Good to see you. You've been busy, I see."

"You noticed? I was giving out some booklets."

"I thought so. But how in the world did you get so many people to take them and read them?"

He said, "It really wasn't so hard. I smiled at each person and said, 'In a lonely city where hope has died, I'd like to give you a personal message of hope from me.' Except for a couple of people, they all took the booklets and most are reading them."

That short train ride was a watershed experience for me. Will taught me that people may seem closed off, but even strangers may open up to us if we demonstrate the kind of gracious, creative caring Will had shown. My heart was stirred by the power of a love that could reach into the lives of these commuters—total strangers to Will. I wanted the same love in my life.

In the years since, I've asked God to use me in the same kind of way. And since I now ride planes more than trains, I ask my friends to pray that I will love the strangers on my plane trips.

I have been amazed to see how God has answered those prayers by arranging for Rose Marie and me to share our faith with total strangers. I couldn't have done a better job if I had scheduled these appointments myself. As we share our faith, it is clear that it is God who is scheduling our airplane meetings. It is God's love that draws people to us and God's love that speaks to their hearts as we talk.

A great example of God's scheduling happened on a hot August day a couple of years ago. Rose Marie and I had landed in New York's Kennedy Airport and were stuck on the runway waiting for our shuttle flight to take off to Philadelphia. I was sitting next to Barry and his adult son. In response to my questioning, he told me about his car dealership in Florida.

"How is it going?" I asked. "I hope it's going well."

"Well, yes," said Barry. "We've had some tight times but lately the business is really doing all right. Thanks for asking."

"My pleasure," I answered. "I'm a pastor, and I have an interest in the success of the businesses in my community. I pray for them to do well. We need the local businesses to succeed. We are in this together."

Barry was moved. He said, "That's great. I never heard of anyone doing that."

When I told Barry that I would pray for his business, he was so touched that he had difficulty speaking. But I could see he also had questions. Why would a stranger care about his business?

To this point I had said nothing about Christ or salvation, but now it was natural to talk about

the Lord's work in my life. In answer to his un-
spoken question, I told him that I hadn't always
been concerned for others. I told him that I was
a former rebel and sinner and that Christ had
died for me and my sins. I said, "He took them
away through his death, and who can be selfish
and self-centered after being loved like that?"

In the meantime others on the plane were listening. Suddenly the man directly across the
aisle leaned over and whispered, "I'm Mike. Listen, after you talk with them, please talk with
me. I want to confess my sins."

I was startled. I finished my conversation
with Barry and turned to the man across the
aisle. Soon he was telling me in a low voice about
the things he felt guilty about. He had overheard
the gospel, but now I explained it to him again. I
told him that faith in Jesus would take away his
sins no matter what he had done. I explained
that Christ takes away sins, not me. Mike confessed his sins over a period of several minutes.
I prayed with him, and he received Christ, trusting his blood to pay for his sins.

The flight was only forty-five minutes long. I
usually like to spend much more time than that
talking to someone about Christ. However, I believe in a sovereign God. He brought these men
across my path, and they heard the message of
redemption. They also felt the touch of the Holy
Spirit. He gave me a love for them that was
clearly from him.

Sometimes God's appointments don't seem so well planned—at least at first. Once Rose Marie and I were flying to Florida to speak, and the plane was delayed on the ground for two hours. To make up for the delay the airline supplied free drinks to everyone. The large man seated next to me downed several, and he then became quite loud and aggressive. I didn't want to be near him, much less share my faith.

However, I had asked my friends to pray for this trip, and Rose Marie and I had been praying as well. So we introduced ourselves and learned that his name was Gerald. Soon, lubricated with a couple more drinks, he told us that he lived in an exclusive area not far from our home.

Gerald mentioned that he was on the board of an area church. We knew of the church and Gerald hastened to tell us how he ran things there. He said, "The minister and the other board members don't have good judgment, but I have all the money, so that improves their judgment. I tell it to them like it is, and they don't have any choice. They go along. I do a lot of good for people, and give away a lot of money."

As he talked, it all clicked. This was one of the wealthiest men in our community and an influential philanthropist. For at least thirty minutes we listened quietly as he told us about his virtues. He seemed to have an endless list.

Finally I said to him, "Well, if you have done all those good things and don't have any real faults, you sure are a lot better than I am. But let me ask you a question," I added. "You do all these good things, but how do you get along with your neighbors? Do you love them?"

He replied, "I sure do. I bought all the houses on my block and rent them to the people I choose. I like all the people I choose and they like me. My neighbors and I get along just fine."

"But neighbors aren't just people you can choose," I pointed out. "What about enemies, people who wrong you? Neighbors include people who may not like you—enemies. I find I can't love them without God's help. Can you?"

This last question slowed him down just a bit, but by this time I was exhausted. So I whispered to Rose Marie, "You take over."

She said quietly to Gerald who was perspiring heavily, "I don't think you know yourself very well. I have listened to you tell us all about your good works. You gave us a long list without repeating yourself. The problem is that God tells us in the Bible that all our righteousness is as filthy rags. All those good deeds won't get you into heaven. Nobody is as good as you say you are. Look, I can really hate people if they cross me and wrong me. I need to ask Jesus for grace to forgive them."

Now the war was on. For a couple of hours, we kept confessing our weaknesses and sins, and Gerald kept confessing his virtues. But he also often repeated what we said about the gospel, loudly disagreeing with it. The ironic thing was that his commanding voice was telling our whole section of the plane the message of the cross.

At last the plane was airborne. Gradually Gerald began to listen more and talk less. By the time we had landed in Orlando, he had heard the whole gospel message.

At the end, Rose Marie said to him with deep concern, "You know, if you die trusting in your virtues and good works, you will end up in hell. And we do not want you to do that. Please, please listen to Jesus."

When the plane landed and taxied to a stop, Gerald grabbed his carry-on bag and headed for the door like a projectile out of a cannon. But he did not escape before I had given him a pamphlet with our church's name and address. Then, before the other passengers could move, I quickly stood up and said to those sitting nearby, "I know you heard most of our conversation, and you now know what we believe. In case you want to hear more, here is the same pamphlet that Gerald took."

Faces were smiling and several hands reached out for the pamphlets. I know that they were able to take them instead of retreating in suspicion because they had heard Rose Marie and me confess many of our weaknesses. We have made a conscious effort to move with humility into the lives of other people, to love them from below, rather than from above. Our weaknesses have become our point of contact, and this openness and vulnerability causes people to open up to us in return. But Gerald was very much afraid of the kind of openness he saw in us.

Gerald later called our church and asked questions about Rose Marie and me and our ministries. His heart seemed stirred although I do not know if he ever accepted our message of salvation through faith instead of good works. But another passenger on the plane, who had taken one of the pamphlets, wrote to say that our conversation on the plane had renewed his faith.

That is just one of many opportunities that God has given me to share my faith as I travel. Another time I was sitting next to a manager of a large corporation. He was friendly, and we talked over coffee on a two-hour flight. After he spent some time telling me about himself, his work, and his family, he asked me, "And what do you do?"

I smiled and said, "I go around the world helping people in trouble, but I also do a lot of blundering. Then I write books about it."

I immediately had his attention, and he began to ask me questions. I explained, "There was a time when I had a very high opinion of my own perfection and righteousness. But I had an eight-year-long conflict with my daughter, Barbara. At the beginning of our estrangement, I saw all the faults on her side, but gradually I came to see myself as pretty badly flawed. When I admitted my failings, it eventually freed her to admit hers. This brought about a wonderful reconciliation between us."

I continued telling him about my daughter and the book we had written together, *Come Back, Barbara.* I said, "You hear people talk about sin, but most people don't really understand what the word means. They hear the word 'sin,' and they often think it means sexual lust. That *is* sin, but sin is something deeper. It is my wanting to control Barbara, and her rebelling against me. It's living for yourself and fighting against God's will. It's really trying to be a little god and to run your own life your own way. In families, it expresses itself in the clash of big egos. This is what causes conflicts."

Then I talked for a time about the atoning death of Christ: "It's easy to underestimate the power of Christ's sacrifice if you underestimate God's holiness and our sin. Our sin comes from our rebellious, self-centered hearts. God is holy all the way, and he hates sin. So you see our danger if we die without having Christ."

I ended by saying, "I know that the cross of Christ is my only hope. There he took my judgment upon himself. He died for me. I know I'm completely forgiven. Faith is poor sinners like me getting desperate and entrusting themselves to Jesus as their only hope."

We sat there quietly for a time. I eventually broke the silence by asking, "Do you see yourself as ready to turn from your sins and trust your life to Christ?"

He looked thoughtful and I waited. He then said, "While you were talking I did that."

I was surprised. This was definitely different from sharing my faith in a boarding house. But this man said that as I talked about Christ, he found himself believing, and so he had given his life to Christ.

During the remainder of the flight we talked more about the gospel. I liked what I heard. His turn to Christ seemed genuine and childlike. He had a church background, but he said this was the first time anyone had explained to him what salvation was all about. We also talked about how the Christian life goes forward by constantly going to the cross to be cleansed from our sins. I gave him some literature and later sent him a copy of *Come Back, Barbara*.

I certainly had stories to tell the friends who had prayed for me. I had asked them to pray that the Father would bring across my path persons he had prepared. I also asked them to pray that the Father would give me the wisdom, love, and humility to speak honestly from the standpoint of my weaknesses.

Throughout my life God had taught me the supreme importance of believing that I do not meet people by accident. It is part of his wise and perfect plan, and I can be confident of this as I speak to them. He has also shown me that love is expressed through careful and sympathetic listening. This opens up strangers like nothing else.

Now I was learning more from the Lord. Usually when we talk to strangers, we try to impress them with our accomplishments. We think that if we can impress them, they will listen to what we have to say. But Rose Marie and I find that sharing our weaknesses is what catches the attention of strangers. Then they are willing to listen to how God has changed us.

They also feel the touch of the Holy Spirit. He gives us a love for them that we don't have on our own. All this happens because we ask people to pray.

Humility comes to us as we ask people to pray for us, and as we grow in dependence on Christ's work on the cross. When we ask God for humility, he gives it to us, and other people are attracted to us. The Father then uses our humility to convict the consciences of Christians and non-Christians alike. I have seen the Spirit work powerfully in this way on many occasions.

This is the prayer I have often prayed for myself and others: "Father, we confess that we are naturally self-centered and self-exalting. Any humility we have is the gift of your Holy Spirit. Please, please touch us now with a humble heart, and break our pride and self-dependence. Make us feel our weakness and your strength. Then give us a loving boldness in witness that is only from you."

God loves to answer this prayer with a *yes!*

Epilogue by
Rose Marie Miller

CHAPTER TEN

Jenkintown, Pennsylvania, 1998

Jack planned to finish this book with stories of how he shared his faith in hospitals both as a visiting pastor and as a sick patient. But he wasn't able to complete this before his final hospitalization for open-heart surgery. Since I knew the material that he wanted to share, I decided to incorporate some of it into an epilogue for this book.

As a young pastor Jack spent a lot of time visiting the sick and sharing the good news of the gospel with those too weak to do anything but listen. Through an amazing experience early in his ministry he learned that even a comatose person could hear and respond to the message of salvation.

One day when Jack was a young pastor in California, he received an unexpected call from the hospital. Jack had known the man's health wasn't good, but he wasn't prepared for this message: "Come to the hospital quickly. Mr. York is dying!"

At the hospital Jack received his second shock. The sound of Mr. York's breathing was horrible. This non-Christian man was dying from lung congestion; he was suffocating and had already lapsed into a coma.

Jack said, "The whole scene left me dismayed. My impression was of tubes and hospital paraphernalia everywhere. Here I was a young pastor who had never been plunged into anything like this before. To top it off, I didn't know the patient all that well. Once or twice I had talked to him about Christ, but his response had been vague. So what should I do? How do you minister to a man who seems unconscious? No seminary course had prepared me for anything like this."

He wrote about his encounter with Mr. York, "I was convinced that God's sovereign plan governs everything. But what kind of web was the Lord weaving here? When I leaned my heart on the Almighty, the deep waters of death seemed less threatening. Then God began to bring to mind things I'd heard from a Christian nurse when I was a student at San Francisco State.

"She said, 'Don't assume that a person in a coma or apparently unconscious is beyond all communication. Sometimes the patient who does not speak or show signs of listening can still hear you. Don't be misled by appearances.' Then she gave me some specific guidelines to follow:

"1. Read to the patient a short, familiar passage of Scripture, a few verses that sum up the gospel (John 3:16).

"2. Speak rather loudly and briefly, close to the patient's ear.

"3. Repeat the process several times, using as much as you can the very same words each time you speak."

With these thoughts in Jack's mind, he asked Mrs. York's permission to speak with her husband about his need for Christ—and to speak loudly. She consented and Jack read Scripture very loudly and fired off a two-minute sermon setting forth the way of salvation. He did this repeatedly.

For a short time, hope was renewed for Mr. York's recovery, but his life energy continued to drain away. Then, suddenly, a few days later, Mr. York raised up in bed, tubes and all, and said, "Tell Bob I'm saved!" Then he slipped back into the coma. The next day he died. Mrs. York said "Bob" was a Christian neighbor who had been sharing the gospel with her husband.

This experience had a tremendous impact on Jack. Now even the comatose heard the irresistible message of grace from him. Many seriously ill people found hope as Jack told them about the forgiving love of the Father and the sacrificing love of the Son.

But in 1983, Jack's hospital ministry changed dramatically. Since 1979 he had spent a portion of every year preaching and teaching in Uganda. The country, ravaged by the brutal dictatorship of Idi Amin, needed spiritual renewal desperately.

Jack loved Uganda and its people, so every time he had a break from seminary, he was in Africa preaching and teaching. It was here in 1983 that he suffered a major heart attack. Now others needed to pray and care for him.

I remember when the call came on Friday morning, July 1, 1983, the day before Jack was scheduled to leave Kampala for home. Our son-in-law Bob Heppe, who was with Jack in Africa, was on the line. He said, "Mom, Dad has had a heart attack. He is in Nsymbia Hospital."

I arrived in Kampala, July 4. I was so glad to see Jack—white-faced, weak, but alive. He had survived the first three days and he was going to live. He told me later, "The pain was so intense that I couldn't remember any verses from the Bible and I couldn't pray. *I was a weak man.*"

Since he was too weak even to hold up the Bible, he asked his nurses to read to him from the book of Romans. They read, "God presented him [Christ] as a sacrifice of atonement, through faith in his blood. He did this to demonstrate his justice" (Romans 3:25 NIV).

"Do you know what this means?" he asked them. They did not. He continued, "Take the

Bible home and read this chapter and then we will talk about it some more." To say this much took all of Jack's strength.

As they continued to read the Bible to him each day, the nurses began to see their own need for a Savior. Living and working in a country with so much confusion and cruelty—the terrible legacy left by Amin—they were ready to hear that God loved them. One nurse after another trusted in Christ's blood to make her righteous before a holy God. Their singing and praying attracted other nurses who had a hunger for a new life. A little church was formed in that room. Jack's church planting was extended to the Nsymbia Hospital!

The same grace that changed these young women also gave Jack strength. Soon he was sitting in a wheelchair outside in the hospital grounds, sharing his faith with an ill and very distraught Hindu.

Jack said, "I will pray for you that God will heal you, but I will pray in the name of Jesus Christ, the Son of God, who is not one of your gods." He kept repeating this as he talked to the man. After many similar conversations, the man put his faith in Christ and was healed. Jack repeated, "Now who are you going to say healed you?" The Indian replied, "Jesus Christ healed me, the Son of the Living God."

We stayed in Uganda for a month before Jack was able to travel home to the U.S. His recovery was slow and steady. He was able to continue to preach and teach, and was soon traveling to other churches to do the same. He also wrote *Come Back, Barbara* with our daughter Barbara, a story of their estrangement and reconciliation.

During these years Jack and our son Paul developed a training course in Christian living called the Sonship Course. The heart of the course is what Jack had learned over the years: living out of the power and strength of the Spirit to apply the gospel to our lives. The course was (and is) used for renewal in churches both here and abroad. In the midst of all this, Jack faced another major health crisis.

On October 8, 1987, we sat together in a room at Germantown Hospital in Philadelphia. "Jack," the doctor said, "you have cancer." Keren, our daughter, and I were on either side of his bed, listening to these life-threatening words. We knew they were coming. We had just been with the radiologist, a friend, in the hospital lunch room. He told us about the cancer. But it was still a shock to hear the doctor's words.

"The tumor is massive, pressing against other organs. Your kidneys have ceased to function. Unless they start to function you will not be able to take chemotherapy." The doctors knew Jack's weakened heart could not handle the strain of the kidney failure and the growing cancer.

Jack later wrote, "The temptation for me was to be overwhelmed by fear and passively give up the fight, even perhaps turning away from God to lapse into numbness, self-pity, and fear."

Prayer was mobilized for him. People all around the world prayed for his recovery.

After surgery Jack had to be moved to the Coronary Care Unit. All his systems were failing. But as Jack was being wheeled into CCU, he was still sharing his faith with his nurse. Too weak to go on, he handed Barbara's husband, Angelo, the "New Life" Booklet, and said, "You take over now." Angelo gladly continued telling the nurse about Jesus.

Jack spent four days in the Coronary Care Unit, hooked up to life-support systems. He experienced peace amid the waves of weakness. While many people prayed, his kidneys started to function, and chemotherapy was started.

One of the nurses in CCU told Jack about her estranged daughter. Jack shared with her the story of our daughter Barbara's estrangement and reconciliation. He used this story to share the gospel with the nurse.

That same nurse recently wrote me a note at Christmas, ten years after she met Jack in the CCU. "Your husband always gave me hope that my daughter would come home. I am sorry that he isn't here so I could tell him that she finally came home in March. She and her husband presented me with my first granddaughter. Just wanted you to know."

Other nurses and doctors were also touched

by Jack's faith. They would come to his room ready to minister to him. Instead they left with a large dose of the healing power of the gospel.

God restored Jack to active life and ministry after six months of chemotherapy. Once again we were flying around the world: preaching the gospel in the U.S., Europe, and Africa; recruiting and overseeing missionaries; and spending time writing.

Our travels came to another abrupt halt in March of 1995. We were getting ready for bed at home in Jenkintown, Pennsylvania, when Jack said, "Rose Marie, my arm is numb, and my leg is starting to feel strange." We rushed him to Abington Hospital where he gradually regained strength in his arm and leg.

This hospital stay resembled the others. He always expressed his thanks to the nurses and doctors for their care and then moved the conversation to his favorite topic—Jesus. He loved to tell a good story. He gave out copies of my book, *From Fear to Freedom*. He proudly told the hospital staff how I was released from so many fears by God's grace. Jack was, as always, eager to let others in on the good news.

Later a friend of ours met a woman when he was working as a disc jockey in a restaurant. As their talk turned to spiritual things, she mentioned that she had only met one Christian that she liked. It was a stroke patient she had nursed at Abington Hospital. He was always so sweet, she said, and his faith was so real. She had never met anyone like him. His name? Jack Miller.

A major heart attack, life-threatening cancer, and a stroke were stark reminders to Jack that he was a weak man. Through these major health crises Jack learned to know and rely on the love God had for him. This truth, and living for God's glory, became his passion. In mid-June, 1995, the doctor gave him permission to travel to London, where he spoke at a conference for a group of English pastors.

A friend wrote about this conference, "Jack's stroke had followed a particularly powerful sermon that he had preached in Philadelphia. He knew the power that was coming now was risky. But the power came. He was overcome with love and brokenness for the lost. As he preached I became conscious of tears streaming down my face. He wept for a man he knew in Spain, recalling how he had shouted at God to 'Save him, Lord!' In another crescendo I remember him crying out, 'I am a dying man preaching to dying men!' I will never forget that day; the passion, the brokenness, the love for sinners."

Jack's last opportunity to share the life-changing truths of the gospel was in Germany. Despite increasing weakness and angina pains, he preached in February 1996 to a large charismatic church in Hamburg, Germany. His theme was "Awake to God's Glory."

His first message was, "A Broken Son Glorifying the Father." This was now true of Jack. Broken in health (he almost didn't go because of physical weakness), broken by his Father's love, broken by his sin of pride and self-sufficiency, caring no more for his reputation, he preached the riches of Christ.

In each message he centered everything on the glory of the gospel and the sovereignty of the Holy Spirit in reaching the brokenhearted. Jack's speaking was bathed in prayer. The days were long, but when he preached, he was strong.

We returned to Spain where he had been writing a book about his experiences with cancer. But that proved impossible. His angina attacks worsened, and he became progressively weaker. Tests showed that he had two blocked arteries. Travel back to the U.S. was impossible.

It was then that our son Paul said, "Dad, why don't you write a book about the many opportunities God gave you to share your faith?" So, in the last six weeks of his life, this book was written.

Bypass heart surgery was scheduled on Tuesday, April 2, 1996 in Malaga, Spain. Three of our children, Barbara, Paul, and Keren, were with him after his surgery. Roseann and Ruth, our other two daughters, were home mobilizing prayer for his recovery. Remembering how Mr. York heard Jack even in a coma, we prayed, read the Bible, and sang to him whenever we had the opportunity to see him. Thousands of people around the world prayed with us that he would live. Someone said, "If prayer alone could keep Jack alive, he would have lived."

But Jack never left ICU. Two days after surgery, the doctor took him off the ventilator to breathe with an oxygen mask. We told him we loved him. He heard us, because his lips formed the words, "I love you." Those were the only words he spoke during the week. The day after Easter, God brought him to his eternal home.

Once, a dying patient told Jack that she wasn't interested in going to heaven because it would be too boring. Jack asked her, "What was the happiest moment of your life?"

She said, "The best and happiest times of my life came when I was with someone I really loved."

Jack replied, "That is what makes heaven so very special. Jesus is my very best friend. And the great thing about heaven is being there forever with your best and truest friend."

Now Jack is with his best and truest friend. He loved sharing his faith. It is a faith worth sharing.

"A New Life" Booklet

Have you ever felt there was something missing in your life? Something important but you didn't know what? That may be the **new life** God wants you to have. A life of joy, peace, and fulfillment. A life . . . which you can receive today. Carefully consider these **Five Important Facts** . . . and find out how you can get that new life and become a brand-new person.

1   *A loving God sent His Son Jesus into the world to bring you a new and abundant life.*

Jesus said,
"If anyone thirsts, let him come to me and drink. He that believes in me . . . from within him shall flow rivers of living water" (John 7:38–39).

He also said concerning those He loves,
"I came that they might have life and have it abundantly" (John 10:10).

This new life brings you the fruit of the Spirit: "love, joy, peace, patience, kindness, goodness, faithfulness, gentleness, self-control" (Galatians 5:22). **It also gives POWER!**

God's Holy Spirit gives you the power to overcome . . .

feelings of loneliness, stress, fear of people and the future (1 John 4:18).

And the power to break unbreakable habits like . . .

selfishness, depression, uncontrolled anger, prejudice, sexual lust, overeating, overdrinking, drug abuse (1 Corinthians 6:9–11).

But Why Are So Many People Without This New Life?

2 *Because . . . people are self-centered, not God-centered.*

This means that by nature you are spiritually dead and deceived. (Ephesians 2:1: "You were dead through your trespasses and sins.")

TO BE SPIRITUALLY DEAD AND DECEIVED is to be centered on yourself and not on your Creator, and to believe . . .

A Big Lie

People show this, according to Romans 1:21–31, by being . . .

> unthankful to God, perverted, greedy, jealous, bitter, proud, mean, devious, foolish.

Since man's first sin, he has tried to be INDE-PENDENT of God. Actually each human being is entirely DEPENDENT on God for breath, food, health, shelter, physical and mental abilities. THE BIG LIE: SELFISH INDEPENDENCE:

> self-trust, self-boasting, self-reliance, self-analysis, self-hating, self-seeking

3 *Self-centered man is separated from a holy God by three big barriers.*

Bad Record
Romans 3:23
"All have sinned . . ."

Bad Heart
Mark 7:21
"From the heart of man come evil thoughts . . ."

Bad Master
John 8:34
"Whoever commits sin is a slave . . ."

. . . consequences of sin as separation from God. "The wages of sin is death" (Romans 6:23a).

Now

1. A dry, thirsty, unsatisfied life.
2. A guilty, accusing conscience (depression, fears, etc.).
3. An aging body that must shortly die.

To Come

1. Loss of all friendship and earthly joys forever (Matthew 8:12).
2. Frightful pains of body and conscience forever (Mark 9:48).
3. Dreadful thirst of soul and body forever (Luke 16:19–31).

4 God's Solution! No Barriers!

Perfect Record

1 Corinthians 1:30
"Christ . . . is made our righteousness."

New Heart

Ezekiel 36:25–26
"A new heart I will give you."

Good Master

Matthew 11:28–30
"My yoke is easy."

"The blood of Jesus, God's Son, cleanses us from all sin" (1 John 1:7).

The Benefit of Jesus' Death . . .
Love's Biggest Gift

"The free gift of God is eternal life through Jesus Christ" (Romans 6:23). Jesus, the God-man, is the biggest gift of the Father's love. On the cross Jesus suffered all the torments of hell as a substitute for His people (John 3:16; 10:15). He was legally condemned by God as their representative, removing the barriers of a bad record, a bad heart, and a bad master. The Father's love can do no more. Risen from the dead, Jesus now lives to give you a new record, a new heart, Himself as a new master—and the free gift of eternal life now!

You Need to Make Sure

God says you either have a NEW LIFE or you are a lawbreaker DEAD in your self-centeredness. Are you personally alive or dead? If you are still dead, you need to know . . .

5 *How to receive the Lord Jesus into your life . . .*

1. Turn . . .

in sorrow from your sins: "Let the wicked forsake his way, and the unrighteous man his thoughts; let him turn to the Lord, that He may have mercy on him, and to our God, for He will abundantly pardon" (Isaiah 55:7).

2. Trust . . .
in Christ Jesus alone: "Believe in the Lord Jesus Christ and thou shalt be saved, and thy house" (Acts 16:31).

Repentance is . . . not our suffering or our good works to earn our salvation, but a turning from our sins to the living God through Jesus Christ.

Trust in the Lord Jesus is . . . accepting, receiving, and resting on Him alone as the Savior from our sins.

Begin a *NEW LIFE*
Will you now surrender your life to Christ by turning from your self-centered way and trusting in Him alone? Here is a guideline to help you confess your sins and come to know God through taking the Lord Jesus Christ as your **own** personal Savior:

> "Heavenly Father, I am really a selfish person. I have wanted my own way—not yours. I have often been jealous, proud, and rebellious. You are my Creator, but I have acted as though I was lord of all. I have not been thankful to you. I have not

listened to your Word the Bible and have not loved your Son. But now I see that all my sin is against you. I now repent of this evil attitude. I turn from all my sins and trust that Jesus shed His precious blood to cleanse me from all my guilt. I now receive Him as my Savior and Lord of my life."

I, _____, turn from my sins and take Christ as my Lord and Savior. By His help I promise to obey Him in every part of my life.

How Does This New Life Continue?
The same way it began—in faith and prayer.

1. **Pray constantly.** Prayer is talking to God. Keep doing it all the time. Include in it praise, thanksgiving, confession of sins, petitions for others' salvation, and requests for help.
2. **Read your Bible.** Study your Bible every day. It is the food for your new life and your sure guide. In it you meet Jesus and learn to claim His promises for your life.
3. **Worship with others.** Meet with a church where the Bible is taught and obeyed and where Jesus Christ is Lord and Savior.

4. **Witness to others.** Tell your friends what Christ has done for you—and wants to do for them. Be tactful and back up your words by improvement in manners and doing deeds of kindness.

This booklet has been designed to introduce you to Jesus Christ, the author of eternal life. If it has been helpful to you and you have questions or comments, contact:

World Harvest Mission
100 West Ave. W960
Jenkintown, PA 19046-2697

Phone: (215) 885-1811
Fax: (215) 885-4762
E-mail: info@whm.org

Additional copies of this booklet for sharing Christ with others are available by contacting:

Westminster Media
Phone: (800) WTS-TAPE
E-mail: wtsmedia@compuserve.com

New Life Presbyterian Church and World Harvest Mission

In the winter of 1972 Jack and Rose Marie Miller started a prayer meeting in their home. About a dozen people gathered in their living room every Sunday afternoon. As the group grew, they added worship and Bible teaching to the prayer meeting. The group quickly became too large for the Miller's home and had to move to their own facilities. In 1974 it officially became New Life Presbyterian Church. As the church continued to grow, Jack Miller was able to realize his vision for church planting both at home and abroad. The original New Life Presbyterian Church has planted two daughter churches, and both of them have also planted churches. There is now a network of five New Life churches in the Philadelphia area.

World Harvest Mission was organized by Jack Miller as part of the missions outreach of New Life Presbyterian Church. Church leaders from New Life and other congregations who shared

Jack's vision gathered with him to work together in wider ministry. After many informal missions to Ireland and Uganda, World Harvest was officially established in 1983. Today, more than one hundred people serve on four continents. World Harvest is committed to bringing renewal to churches both here and abroad and to planting churches abroad. The mission's vision is *the power of the gospel leading to renewal and missions.* After Jack's death in 1996, Rev. Steve Smallman became the executive director. Although Jack is gone, his legacy of joyfully sharing the gospel is continued by the many men and women who serve with World Harvest Mission.

For more information contact:

World Harvest Mission
100 West Ave. W960
Jenkintown, PA 19046-2697

Phone: (215) 885-1811
Fax: (215) 885-4762
E-mail: info@whm.org
Website: www.whm.org